# The Journey Begins

You will be taking a spiritual journey of discovery, adventure, and growth as you read this book. Making soul contact and awakening your heart centers can be one of the most important and transformative journeys you will ever take. As you awaken your heart centers, you can receive all the gifts of your soul, such as its serenity, strength, clarity, joy, power, light, and vision. You can learn to love and accept yourself as unconditionally as your soul loves and accepts you.

As you awaken your heart centers you are making an important contribution to humanity. You are adding to the vibration of love that will assist others in awakening their heart centers. All problems facing humanity—hunger, war, poverty, crime, homelessness, and environmental damage—will be solved when enough people have made soul contact and have awakened heart centers. Then people will cooperate, share, and work together for the good of the whole, and solutions will be found.

I offer you the information in this book as a guide to assist you on your journey of experiencing all the love within you that is waiting to unfold. As with many journeys, it may only be after you return that you realize how much you have done and how different you are from when you started. This journey begins and ends with love, for love is the most powerful energy in the universe. —Orin

# Books by Sanaya Roman

Earth Life Series

**Living With Joy:**
*Keys to Personal Power and Spiritual Transformation*

**Personal Power Through Awareness:**
*A Guidebook for Sensitive People*

**Spiritual Growth:**
*Being Your Higher Self*

Soul Life Series

**Soul Love:**
*Awakening Your Heart Centers*

# Books by Sanaya Roman and Duane Packer, Ph.D.

**Opening to Channel:**
*How to Connect With Your Guide*

**Creating Money:**
*Keys to Abundance*

Book I of the Soul Life Series

# Soul Love

## Awakening Your Heart Centers

An Orin Book
Sanaya Roman

H J Kramer
TIBURON, CALIFORNIA

H J Kramer Inc
P. O. Box 1082
Tiburon, CA 94920

Editor: Nancy Grimley Carleton
Editorial Assistants: Linda Merrill, Claudette Charbonneau
Cover Art: Debra Ross / On-Line Graphics
Cover Design: Jim Marin / Marin Graphic Services
Production: Schuettge and Carleton
Composition: David Duty / LaserGraphics
Manufactured in the United States of America.
10  9  8  7  6  5  4  3  2  1

Library of Congress Cataloging-in-Publication Data

Orin (Spirit)
    Soul love : awakening your heart centers / [channeled
through] Sanaya Roman.
        p. cm. — (Soul life series . 1)
    ISBN 0-915811-77-4
    1. Spirit writings.  I. Roman, Sanaya.  II. Title.  III. Series.
BF1301.O722 1997
133.9′3—dc21
                                                    97-19845
                                                        CIP

# DEDICATION

This book is dedicated to all of you who are making soul contact and awakening your heart centers, for the contribution you are making to humanity as you do.

—Orin and Sanaya

# To Our Readers

The books we publish are our contribution to an emerging world based on cooperation rather than on competition, on affirmation of the human spirit rather than on self-doubt, and on the certainty that all humanity is connected. Our goal is to touch as many lives as possible with a message of hope for a better world.

—Hal and Linda Kramer, Publishers

# CONTENTS

# In Appreciation

I want to thank all of you who have read Orin's books, listened to his tapes, or come to his seminars, for your support of Orin's work and for spreading his messages of hope and love to others. In addition, I want to thank all of you who joined me at the soul level as Orin brought through this book. I have felt your love and support often.

A big thank-you to Duane Packer and his guide DaBen, for the value I have received from your teachings in how to awaken my light body, and for all your contributions to this book.

My heartfelt gratitude to Edward Alpern for the many hours he spent with Orin and me on this book, holding a space, taking notes, and assisting us in numerous ways.

I want to thank Hal and Linda Kramer for their vision, flexibility, and support of Orin's work. Besides being wonderful to work with, their lives are inspiring and their friendship is a treasured gift. Thank you also to their staff, Jan Phillips and Mick Laugs, for their many contributions to the publishing of this book.

Thank you to my sister Debra for her wonderful, inspired cover artwork that portrays the energy of the heart centers. She is a gifted artist whose art reaches within and touches our spirit, lifting us to a higher plane simply by its viewing.

I am grateful to Nancy Carleton for her helpful suggestions

and gentle editing, to Linda Merrill for her editing assistance, and to David Duty for his typesetting.

I want to thank JoAnn Johnson and Gloria Dozier for their many contributions to the LuminEssence office. Both have brought much light to my life and to the lives of others, and freed me to write this book.

A warm acknowledgment to my family and friends for all the opportunities they have provided me to learn soul love. My mother's passing during the writing of this book taught me that love is the most important gift we give to others. Thanks to my dad, Court Smith, and all my brothers and sisters and nieces and nephews for their contributions to my life.

I want to thank Neera Paine of Mt. Shasta, California, for her excellent body and energy work which supported me as I wrote this book, and Carol Erickson for her wise counsel. A special thank-you to LaUna Huffines for our play together in the higher realms that has opened many doorways.

I was often guided by Orin to open certain books that would confirm the information he had given me or clarify subtle points he wanted to make. The Alice A. Bailey books have been of great value, and I want to offer my profound thanks and gratitude to Lucis Trust for making the books available. I highly recommend any of the Alice Bailey books.

With deep gratitude, I thank all the distributors and their staffs, as well as all the committed, dedicated bookstore owners and their employees whose loving service makes it possible for these books to reach you.

Finally: To all my family, friends, students, and colleagues; you are my inspiration and my teachers. I send all of you light and blessings.

# Preface by Sanaya

Sanaya (pronounced Sah-nay-ah): I welcome all of you who are reading this book. If this is your first Orin book, I am delighted you are joining us in awakening your heart centers and learning more about soul love. If you have read other Orin books, I am glad to have this opportunity to join you again as you take another step on your path of spiritual growth.

This book was "given" to me by a nonphysical guide who calls himself Orin. People often ask who Orin is. When I ask Orin, he replies that who he is does not matter; what is important is the message he brings and how useful that message is to you. He wants the focus to be on you and your growth, not upon himself.

I experience Orin as a being of great love, wisdom, and compassion. He never tells people what to do or how to live their lives. When asked, Orin will offer suggestions and ideas to assist people in seeing more choices. He has a constant message: that the universe is friendly, that it is unlimited in its abundance, that everything is happening perfectly for our good although we may not always understand why, and that we can choose to grow through joy rather than through struggle. He encourages you to accept only the ideas presented that seem true to the deepest part of your being, and to set aside any that do not.

Orin tells me he is a Being of Light. He says he is working with us at this time because humanity is going through a major transition and awakening. Orin has lived an earth life and is aware of the many challenges of living on the earth plane. He says that he now "lives" on the soul plane and in even higher realms. One of his purposes is to serve humanity. Part of his service is to offer people a path of spiritual growth and to assist people in reaching their higher self and soul. In this book he is offering you a way to awaken your heart centers and to live in your soul's rhythm of love, serenity, and oneness.

I am in a relaxed, yet alert state of awareness when I bring Orin's messages through me. I am fully present and aware of both my own thoughts and his. When Orin is with me, I do not feel as if I am in a trance state; my voice does not change, nor do I lose consciousness. Orin says he communicates with me through a form of higher telepathy. He impresses my soul and higher mind with messages that are then received into my conscious awareness. Orin says that although his energy and light are available to any who call upon him, he will not bring messages and information through other channels until after my lifetime.

Orin's words express only a fraction of what I am experiencing. There is a richness of feelings, pictures, and illumination transmitted with them that is beyond description. I feel his contact as if I have expanded into a world of light and joy. It is as if through Orin I can experience a world of increased understanding, greater awareness, and more compassion and love. The ability to reach this state of awareness is an ability that everyone possesses. It is a matter of listening, opening, and allowing yourself to expand beyond the "you" that you know as your normal awareness. It involves letting your identity grow into one that includes a more expansive perspective. Many of you experience this when you are doing work you love and feel clearer, wiser, and more inspired than in your normal state of awareness. Some call this expanded state channeling, inspiration, creative thinking, intuitive insight, or expanded awareness.

Several years ago, after finishing the book *Spiritual Growth: Being Your Higher Self*, the third book of the Earth Life Series, Orin told me he wanted to write a book called *Soul Love*. It would be the first book of the Soul Life Series, a collection of books teaching people how to live as their soul. *Soul Love* would teach people how to love as their soul, to awaken their heart centers, and to create soul relationships. *Soul Love* sounded like a wonderful topic, and I looked forward to beginning.

However, it seemed that Orin had other things in mind. I had been offering classes on creating abundance with a man named Duane Packer. We were also teaching people how to connect with a guide. We had made the information we taught in classes available through the books *Creating Money: Keys to Abundance* and *Opening to Channel: How to Connect With Your Guide*. After the book *Spiritual Growth* was published, Orin and Duane's guide, DaBen, wanted us to start teaching a new course in spiritual transformation called Awakening Your Light Body. This course teaches people how to expand their consciousness to experience the higher dimensions of light. People then learn how to bring light from the higher dimensions into their daily lives, and to use it to transform their physical body, emotions, mind, and daily reality.

I kept wondering when Orin would tell me it was time to start the *Soul Love* book. When I asked, Orin would tell me to keep expanding my consciousness through awakening my light body. Awakening my light body increased my sensitivity to the subtle energies of my soul, the higher dimensions, and the Beings of Light. Finally, several years later, Orin told me it was time to begin *Soul Love*.

I had several hundred sessions with Orin to bring through the information contained in this book. Some information also comes from Orin meditations, talks, and teachings given over a ten-year period. As Orin and I worked on this book, we spent many hours in meditation. We connected with the souls of all of you who would be awakening your heart centers, and who wanted this soul connection with Orin and me. I felt the joy of this connection as I channeled and wrote. You have come to seem like my family on the soul plane. I already know a few of you; however, there are many of you whom I have not met in person. Although I may not know your face or name, I do know the beauty and light of your soul.

As I connected with my soul and awakened my heart centers through using the processes you will learn, my life changed in many ways. Although I thought my life was fine before I started, I came to realize it could be even better than I had imagined. As I felt my soul's power, presence, and love, I gained a greater trust and confidence in myself and in the universe. Awakening my heart centers taught me new ways to love others that were more empowering than my old ways. As I connected with other people's souls, my relationships changed for the better.

I look forward to joining you on the soul plane as you read this book. My soul will be present in the group of souls you will be guided to connect with as you continue. Together we will join others to meet and blend with our souls, to awaken our heart centers, and to call upon the Great Ones to awaken the heart centers of humanity. My love is with you as you read this book and embark upon the wonderful journey of awakening your heart centers that lies ahead.

# Introduction by Orin

Greetings from Orin! As you continue, you are doing more than reading a book; you are undertaking a journey of transformation. You are embarking upon a wonderful adventure of meeting your soul and learning to love as your soul does. Many wonderful changes can happen as you read and open to your soul's love and wisdom. You will be planting seeds of growth and expansion that can unfold for weeks and months afterward. Some seeds may sprout immediately, and others may blossom over time.

In Section I, Blending With Your Soul, you will journey to the soul plane where your soul lives. You will receive transmissions from the Beings of Light to assist you in meeting and blending with your soul. As you become aware of the beauty of your soul, you will know how special, unique, and perfect you are. You will discover how to tap into your soul's love, light, will, power, and presence to create wonderful and powerful changes in your life.

In Section II, Awakening Your Heart Centers, you will blend with your soul to awaken your three heart centers. The first is located in an area around your physical heart. I call this your *primary heart center* or *heart center* (singular). The second is the heart of your head center, located in an area near the middle of the top of your head. I call this your *head center*. The final heart center is your *solar plexus center*, located in an area near your navel. I will call this your *solar plexus center*. When all three of these heart centers are working together, you can express a wise, expanded love called *soul love*.

Soul love is a steady, consistent radiation of the Universal Presence of Love that is the very essence of the universe. Soul love is a state of being a part of the oneness—where you are accepted and where you accept, where you are loved and where you love, and where you feel connected to the greater whole of which you are always a part.

*Evolve and expand your love*
*through soul contact.*

As you awaken your heart centers, you can use your expanded love to change your relationships for the better. You can love with a wise heart that empowers others. You can operate from the calm, compassionate, and loving serenity of your soul. You desire to love, and you surrender thoughts, feelings, and behaviors that stand in the way of love. You let go of power struggles, release the barriers to love, and more consistently express soul love.

In Section III, Creating Soul Relationships, you will learn how to love as your soul and to create soul relationships. You will discover how to work with the magnetic love of your soul to attract a soul mate. You will explore finding and fulfilling the higher purposes of your relationships. You will learn how to work with the universal laws of relationship to create what you want in relationships. You will uncover new ways to love yourself and others. You will join with your soul to change aspects of your relationships that no longer serve you. You may choose to release or decrease your involvement with people who do not respond to your love, and draw to you people who do. All your relationships can be loving and supportive; they can all enrich and nourish you.

In Section IV, Receiving and Radiating Love, you will call upon the Great Ones in a celebration of love. You will draw their love into your heart center and become a beacon of love for humanity. You will make wheels of love to be in harmony with your family, friends, and groups of people. You will learn how to work with Masters, Beings of Light, and Enlightened Ones to radiate love to humanity. You will join them to send love to people in need, to children, and to other kingdoms, such as plants, animals, and the earth itself.

Before you continue, you may want to take a moment to close your eyes and make an inner connection with me. I will send you a special transmission of light and love to prepare you to awaken your heart centers. All you need to do is ask for it, and then open to receive my transmission of love. While you are receiving this transmission, affirm that you are willing to know your soul and to love as your soul does.

All you need do is ask if you want to receive transmissions of light, energy, and love from myself and any other Being of Light. From our realm there is no time and space, and we are aware of everyone who contacts us. Anytime you want to receive our transmissions of light, mentally give us your consent. You may sense our energy at those times, or you may have no conscious awareness of it. We will send light to your soul, under its guidance and with its permission.

## $R$ecognize that your soul is a part of you.

Your soul lives on the soul plane. This is a dimension of light and vibration that is closer to Oneness, Source, God, Goddess, the All-That-Is, than the earth plane. Your soul is infused with Spirit. Spirit is the consciousness that permeates and gives life to your soul, just as your soul permeates and gives life to you. Your soul provides the medium through which Spirit can reach you. It is the link between Spirit and your personality.

Your soul is more than a combination of your mental, emotional, and physical bodies. It is the intelligence that directs the building of your bodies. It contains your essence between lifetimes and holds the patterns that created you in this lifetime. It has qualities of mind and mental awareness; it is intelligent and creative. It can draw matter to itself to create forms in your physical world. It lives in higher spiritual dimensions and brings the light and energy of those dimensions to you.

Whenever I refer to your soul, realize that your soul is not separate from you. It is a part of you. As you make soul contact, you are getting to know yourself as a soul. You are expanding your consciousness to experience your soul's greater light, wisdom, and love.

Your soul is made of light and is the embodiment of love. It is a master on its own plane, the soul plane. To grow and fulfill its higher purpose, your soul needs to become a master of the physical plane in which you live. Part of its purpose is to learn how to send its light into your personality, mind, and emotions to establish its higher light and rhythm in all of them. Your personality is your soul as it exists on the earth plane in the world of form and matter. Your level of spiritual evolution is determined by the mastery your soul has gained on the earth plane. Your soul's mastery on the earth plane comes from your ability to become one with it and to know and carry out its goals and purposes.

In other books, I have used the terms *higher self* and *soul* interchangeably. In this book, I will further define higher self as the self who knows and carries out the goals of your soul.

When your personality is fully developed, integrated, and evolved, it becomes an instrument through which your soul can fulfill its goals. It becomes more than a personality; it evolves into your higher self. However, fusion of your mind, emotions, and body—being your higher self—is different from being your soul. Your higher self is a perfect instrument through which your soul can express itself on the earth plane. As your higher self, you carry out the purposes of your soul, instead of following the desires of your personality. You are being your higher self every time you align with your soul and carry out its goals.

To reach enlightenment, you cannot sit around and wait for your soul to contact you and do all the work for you. Your soul is in a state of deep meditation. Most of your soul's attention is turned upward toward the realms of Spirit, of pure God-light, until you are ready to call its attention to you. Although it is always transmitting waves of soul energy to you, its work with you changes when you develop an awareness of it. Then you can use its stimulating, purifying, and transformative energies to grow spiritually.

You are the one who needs to draw your soul's attention to you. You do this through expanding your consciousness, seeking to be your higher self, growing spiritually, and awakening your light body. You draw your soul to you through your will and your intent to make your inner life real. When you consciously connect with your soul and continually draw it into your life, your soul begins to put more attention and energy into you. When this happens, your spiritual growth accelerates rapidly. You work from the earth plane upward, and your soul works from the soul plane downward. As you blend with your soul, you can absorb the spiritual knowledge that is in and around its body. This will improve your daily life. Your soul knows the divine plan for humanity and all life; it knows the part you are to play in that plan.

As your soul sends its light downward, it experiences itself through your earth consciousness. It can more successfully express itself through you as your personality becomes more responsive to it. Your soul can fulfill its higher purpose of mastering and bringing its light into the world of form and matter that you live in. As you blend with your soul and radiate its energy in your daily life, you serve humanity in a valuable way. You become a distributor of soul energy. Through soul contact, you can radiate love, light, beauty, and joy to others.

*Contact your soul and the*
*Enlightened Ones to accelerate*
*your spiritual growth.*

As you continue reading and contact your soul, you will be guided to call upon the Beings of Light to assist you. These Beings include Masters, the Beings of Love, angels, and the Enlightened Ones. All the Beings of Light you will be directed to work with are highly evolved. They can appear to you as male or female, and in many other forms. You may sense them as radiant light, or as having an angelic appearance. They can appear to you as a particular figure or face you might know. They have achieved such a measure of perfection that they no longer need to incarnate in an earth body.

The Beings of Light can live in the world of souls, for there is nothing in the physical world to draw them. Part of their purpose is to serve humanity in its evolution. They do not want your devotion, but instead prefer that you assist them by loving and serving humanity. The Beings of Light work only for the forces of light and good. They surround humanity with their protective aura.

At various times I will suggest that you call upon them to assist you, such as when you call your soul to you, blend with it, and awaken your heart centers. Just as you have assistants and teachers in your realm, there are teachers and assistants in our realm. While you can take all of the steps of making soul contact and awakening your heart centers without calling upon these higher Beings, working with them can make your path of awakening easier and more joyful.

The Beings of Light contact those they work with through mental telepathy. They never take away your free will, interfere with your life, or demand blind obedience. They guide and suggest. They will only come to you when you ask for their assistance and are open to receive it. They make certain thoughts and ideas available to the minds of those who are ready for this contact, those who are focusing on receiving this information, energy, or knowledge. Though these Beings are here to assist you, they will not take away your lessons. They give you support and guidance if you ask for it, and they are always available to offer you love.

# How to Use This Book

There are many ways to read this book. Let your soul show you, through your feelings and desires, which methods are appropriate for you. You can use this book to meet and blend with your soul, enabling you to take a quantum leap in your spiritual growth. You can use this information to change the way you love and to improve your relationships with everyone you know. What you get out of this book will come from your intent, your commitment, and the time and energy you put into using and working with the processes you will learn.

You can read all of this book, or part of it. Because this book offers a step-by-step system of making soul contact and awakening your heart centers, you will gain more if you read the information first in the order it is presented. Each section of the book teaches you new skills, building on the skills you learned in earlier chapters. You can explore each section as long as you want, spending days, weeks, or months before continuing. Or, you may want to read the book straight through, then go back and explore the specific topics that interest you.

The highlighted quotes lead you through most of the key steps in this book. You can use them as you read, and experience the expansion and growth they offer you. You can read them after you finish the book to experience again the transformation these steps can create in your life.

The key processes in each chapter are reviewed in the Soul Play pages that follow each chapter. Practicing these steps after you read the chapter can enhance and deepen your mastery of the skills you just learned. Pick one or more Soul Play steps to play with each day, or choose those that most appeal to you. They can assist you in strengthening your connection to your soul, expressing the qualities of soul love, and improving your relationships.

I have designed the sentences of this book to create rhythm and pauses as you read. This can assist you in experiencing the subtle energies of your soul as you read the sentences and breathe more evenly in a soul rhythm. Explore the spaces the words take you to as ways of developing more awareness of your soul.

*Let the ideas that stand out for you*
*be messages from your soul.*

As you open to your soul, it finds ways to talk to you. After you have read and worked with this book, you may want to open it to any page. Let the information on that page be a message from your soul of what to explore that day.

Allow the process of reading this book to teach you something about how you absorb and integrate new knowledge and experiences. Make everything you do as you read this book the right thing to do. Honor the way you learn and grow. Catch any criticism or judgment of yourself, and replace it with a positive thought of how well you are doing. Part of soul love is loving and respecting yourself. Whether you have dramatic, positive experiences; subtle, slight openings; or no noticeable changes; let all your experiences become the right and perfect ones for you.

As you read, use your imagination to see, picture, imagine, or feel the images. Do not worry if you cannot visualize or picture these images exactly as described. There is no right or wrong way to visualize, feel, sense, picture, or observe your soul or your heart centers. Sensing what is happening is not required for you to reap the benefits of the energies you will receive from your soul and the higher Beings. Use your imagination, and take the time to picture, feel, and discover anything you can. Your imagination is a creative force that can impact matter and create results in your physical world.

As you continue reading, you will learn how to meet and blend with your soul, to awaken your heart centers, and to soul link. Picturing things in your mind as you read can give you an experience of your soul and can assist you in awakening your heart centers. In addition, I have made tapes that take you through many of the processes in the book. These contain transmissions from myself and other Beings of Light who join me in assisting you. (See the back of the book for more information.)

There is more for you to discover about soul love and awakening your heart centers than can be covered in one book. Use this book to stimulate your own inner knowingness and to assist you in discovering your own truths. Accept the truth of these ideas based upon their usefulness and place in your life.

What can be presented as the fullest truth at a particular time in history may later be seen as a fragment of a larger truth when future revelations unfold. The information in this book is complete for now. Yet, as time and the readiness of humanity allow an even higher and expanded picture to emerge, the information in this book will take its place as part of an even larger whole. As you read, go beyond the words and directly experience the energy I am transmitting. This will allow you to grasp parts of that larger truth now.

# Section I

# Blending With Your Soul

*Your personality embarks upon a journey.*
*Solar Light is the guide;*
*the soul plane is the destination.*
*At the Temple of the Enlightened Ones,*
*you call your soul, and it comes.*
*The Beings of Light assist as*
*you blend with your soul.*
*You are infused with the*
*love, will, and light of your soul.*
*Your soul's presence*
*becomes a part of your daily life.*

# Chapter 1

# Preparing Your Personality

*Your higher self contacts your subpersonalities,*
*prepares them for soul contact,*
*and gives them a new vision.*
*Cooperation reigns.*

You are ready to embark upon a wonderful journey of discovery to learn more about yourself and your soul. It is important to prepare your personality for this adventure, just as you would prepare for any journey. If you were going to a new country, you would want to make sure you had the right clothes and equipment, changed your money to the currency of that country, made provisions to be in a place where you might not understand the language, created the time to be there, and prepared mentally for the joys and challenges that lay ahead.

The adventure you are getting ready for is a journey to the soul plane, where you will meet and blend with your soul. You will become familiar with a world made of light, learn a language that is composed of images and is transmitted telepathically, and use a currency of love. You will need to take a break from your daily routines and find a special time to be in this country called the soul plane. As with many journeys, it may only be after you return that you realize how much you have done and how different you are from when you started. Taking this journey to the soul plane and meeting your soul can create many positive shifts in your life. There may be no apparent changes at first. However, connecting with your soul will expand your consciousness, eventually changing the way you think, feel, live, and relate to others. Before you connect with your soul, it is important to take time to look at any fears, doubts, or concerns you may have about doing so.

To resolve any doubts or concerns, you can meet and evolve the various aspects of your personality. Your personality is composed of many parts. For instance, there may be an obedient self, a rebellious self, a parentlike self, a childlike self, a confident self, a fearful self, and so on. I will call these selves *subpersonalities*, or parts of your personality.

You developed most of your subpersonalities when you were young. They decided what was best for you based upon who you were as a child, the environment you found yourself in, and the goals you had at that time. The pictures your sub-personalities have of you and what you want to create may be years out of date! You need to update your subpersonalities whenever you create new goals so that they can cooperate with you to achieve them. They may seem to work against your new goals simply because they are still helping you to achieve older goals that you may no longer want.

For every change you want to make, there are probably one or more subpersonalities who need to be talked to, informed of your plans, and asked to join you in creating this goal. Any time you feel yourself resisting soul contact or any of your goals, take time to discover any subpersonalities whose fears, doubts, and concerns need to be heard and evolved. In this way you gain their cooperation. They can change from resisting what you want to actively assisting you in getting it.

To contact and evolve your subpersonalities, start by relaxing your body. Take a deep breath in. Calm your emotions and quiet your mind. Imagine that you are in a beautiful meadow.

You are your higher self—wise, all-knowing, compassionate, calm, and centered. This is the self who is cooperating with your soul to bring your soul's wisdom to all parts of your personality. It is fine if you are only pretending to be your higher self; it is through using your imagination that you can better know and become your higher self. Picture yourself thinking, feeling, and acting as if you are your higher self.

Let the peace and harmony in the meadow permeate your being. Smell the fragrance of flowers in the air. Feel the gentle breeze. When you are ready, invite into the meadow the part of your personality who needs attention in order to be ready to meet your soul. This can be a subpersonality who may resist soul contact because it is working for other goals. Think of this subpersonality, or call upon any subpersonality who wants to be heard right now. See this subpersonality off in the distance, coming closer to you. Close your eyes and pay attention to what this part looks like. Is it male or female? How old is it? What is it wearing? How is it moving? Notice everything you can about it.

Let this part come close enough to talk to you. It has been wanting to speak to you and is happy you are now willing to talk to it. Ask if it has a name. What does it want to tell you? Take time to listen to this subpersonality. Put this book down, close your eyes, and discover as much about this subpersonality as you can. Feel the unconditional love you as your higher self have for it. Embrace this subpersonality with your love.

Tell this part you are going to take it to the top of a mountain where you will show it an expanded view of your life. Take its hand and travel to this mountaintop. You may walk, dance, or fly to the top. There is a beautiful sun shining above you. The light rays of this sun of transformation begin to change your subpersonality. Notice how it grows more beautiful the higher you go.

This subpersonality is already beginning to grow and change as it walks up the mountain and receives the light of the great sun above you. When you arrive, show this part the expanded view of the horizon—the expanse of the valley below. Let this subpersonality see how much more there is to your life beyond what it has seen up until now.

*Ask your subpersonalities
to assist you in creating your goals.*

As your higher self, turn to face your subpersonality. Ask it what good things it is trying to do for you. All your subpersonalities are trying to assist you, even if they seem to be resisting you. They may be trying to do good things for you based upon old goals or pictures of who you were in the past. Thank this subpersonality for all the good things it is trying to do for you. It wants to be heard and appreciated. Feel it growing more beautiful simply because of your recognition and appreciation of it.

Show this subpersonality your current plans and goals, such as blending with your soul, awakening your heart centers, and expanding your ability to love. Ask this subpersonality if it has any fears of your plans and dreams. Talk to and reassure this part. Tell it that it will still have an important role in your life and ask it to assist you in creating your new plans and dreams. Notice how this part softens, grows, and changes as it gains a new understanding of who you want to be.

Tell this subpersonality that if it wants, you will call upon a Being of Light to evolve it. This Being might be a Master, angel, or guide. This Being knows exactly what to do to evolve your subpersonality. When the subpersonality agrees, a Being of Light joins you. This Being is delighted to be here. Greet this Being and thank him or her for coming. As your higher self, ask this Being for assistance. This Being takes your subpersonality aside and sends it special healing energy. This Being offers your subpersonality love to heal its fears so it can cooperate with you to achieve your goals. You can observe the changes in this self as it evolves, growing more beautiful and mature. Allow it to have as much time with this Being of Light as it needs. When finished, the Being of Light brings your subpersonality back to you. Thank this beautiful Being—this angel, Master, or guide—for the assistance given. This Being acknowledges your thank-you and leaves.

Discover what kind of person the subpersonality has become. What age is it now? How has it changed? Mentally talk to this part. Ask this part if it will now work with you in a way that supports your current goals, visions, and dreams. This is an important step; continue communicating with this subpersonality until it has agreed to cooperate with you. Ask it to be creative and come up with at least three ways to support you in reaching your new goals. You do not need to know what these ways will be. You will simply find it easier to create your plans and dreams. Thank your subpersonality for its cooperation. Both of you are now working together to create your new life.

Imagine the subpersonality standing in front of you. It turns into a symbol of light. Take this symbol into your heart and blend with it. You and your subpersonality have become one. Feel the new light within you as you and your subpersonality join to make soul contact, to awaken your heart centers, and to make your visions, hopes, and dreams a reality.

# Soul Play

Prepare your personality for soul contact by meeting and evolving any subpersonalities who might be resisting taking this step. In addition, if at any time you feel you are resisting soul contact, or are not doing those things you know to be good for you, identify and evolve any subpersonality involved. You can also choose from the following list of subpersonalities who might resist soul contact because they have the following beliefs or feelings:

- Believe they will lose power or control, or no longer be needed.
- Are afraid of having your life change, even if it is for the better.
- Fear that soul contact will make you too powerful, and are afraid of being powerful.
- Assume that living as your soul will take too much effort, and they will not succeed, so why try.
- Worry that people will not love you if you change and grow, or that you will be rejected for being different.
- Are not sure soul contact is the highest goal; perhaps they should wait for something better.
- Are concerned that you might get out of touch with reality and never get practical things done if you lived as your soul.
- Feel undeserving of all the love soul contact can bring, and do not know how to receive that much love.
- Are convinced they can do everything themselves and do not need your soul.

# CHAPTER 2

# Journey to the Soul Plane

*You expand your consciousness with Solar Light
to journey to the soul plane.
In the soul plane you observe
how at every moment you are becoming
a more beautiful and perfect light.*

You are ready to meet and blend with your soul on the soul plane. What is the soul plane? There are many planes of reality, from the physical earth plane you live in to the higher dimensions where everything is made of light. In the earth plane, life force, time, matter, and energy come together in certain ways to form the reality you know. In the soul plane, time is simultaneous, light has a different quality, and matter does not exist as you know it.

You can sense the soul plane and your soul by expanding your consciousness. There are many ways to expand your consciousness to reach the soul plane. They include entering into meditation states, using sound and chanting, and working with a guide. All involve achieving states where your body is relaxed, your emotions are calm, and your mind is clear.

What follows is one way to journey to the soul plane. You do not need to remember each step. All that is important is your intent to reach the soul plane and your sense of the Solar Light.

Focusing on the Solar Light is a powerful and effective way to expand your consciousness to reach the soul plane. What is the Solar Light? It is the soul of the physical sun. People have also called it the Heart of the Sun. It sustains all life on the soul plane, much as your physical sun sustains all life on the earth plane. The Solar Light is a vast, magnificent Being. Its energy reaches into many higher dimensions and shines through to the earth plane. It is the sum total of all consciousness on the soul plane and all planes below it, including the earth plane. The Solar Light is a light of beauty, perfection, and love.

Think of your physical sun and imagine that the Solar Light is like this physical sun, yet even more beautiful and radiant. Since it is the soul of the sun, you need to use your inner eyes and imagination to picture it. You might make a symbol of it in your mind if you cannot sense or feel it. Then, focus upon this symbol as you journey to the soul plane. However, you do not need to be able to make a picture of it, feel it, or do anything other than think of the Solar Light for it to expand your consciousness and guide you to the soul plane.

*Call Solar Light to you
and surround yourself
with its light.*

Going to the soul plane is a journey of expansion instead of a journey of movement. Once you are in the soul plane, you can meet and blend with your soul. Start your journey to the soul plane now by bringing the Solar Light into your awareness. Greet it as a living, loving Being. Picture a stream of love coming from the Solar Light directly into your heart center, located in an area around your physical heart. This stream of love is the energy that world saviors send to humanity through their awakened heart centers. Its magnetic love attracts all to itself. The love being sent from the Solar Light is a force that stirs in the hearts of all people, leading them home to the spiritual realms of light and love.

Put your body in a comfortable position. Adjust your posture so that you feel relaxed. Look upward with your inner eyes, directing your inner sight to the Solar Light. Relax your jaw and the muscles around your eyes. Pay attention to your body and relax any areas of tightness or tension. Let go of your outer world for now. Become aware of your inner world of thoughts and feelings. Release any concerns about how your day is going, or what you need to do next.

Continue to relax and rise to the soul plane by playing with your breathing. Take a deep, easy breath in. Imagine that you are breathing in Solar Light. Then, release your breath gently. Imagine that you are sending Solar Light out to the world with your outbreath. Repeat this several times. Let yourself grow more relaxed with each breath.

Picture your spine as a hollow rod that can hold light. Call Solar Light to you, letting it fill this rod with light. Keep absorbing Solar Light until you have created a pillar of light inside your body that begins to glow. Light spreads out from this pillar into an area around your body, forming a cocoon of light all around you.

Let your light continue to move outward. As it does, imagine that you can sense light in all the material objects and living things around you. Everything in your world is vibrating light. Close your eyes and picture what your environment might look like if you could see everything as light. As you do this you are developing the ability to experience the subtle energies of light as they exist in your three-dimensional world of form and matter.

## *D*raw Solar Light into your DNA
### *to evolve your body.*

As you breathe in Solar Light, send a stream of its light into the DNA in the center of every cell in your body. Imagine you are evolving the code of life within you to take you to your next level of evolution. Your DNA provides the code upon which your body is built. During the moments when you focus upon the Solar Light, the cells being born in your body consist of a finer matter containing more Solar Light.

To experience the soul plane and your soul, your emotions need to become very still, smooth, and flowing. Your emotions look like small, vibrating particles of light that surround and penetrate your physical body. You might picture your emotions as vibrating rapidly when you are in ordinary states of consciousness. They can respond to all the emotional energies about you on the earth plane. In addition, strong emotions or fears can cause your emotional body to vibrate intensely.

To quiet your emotions, breathe calmly as you just did. Think of the Solar Light. Let its rays touch these vibrating particles of your emotional body until they become calm. If you have any worries, concerns, or feelings that are keeping you agitated, imagine Solar Light flowing into them. Sense the vibrating particles of your emotional body growing quieter. You will want to be in a calm and flowing emotional state when you meet and blend with your soul.

You can continue to expand into the soul plane by creating a clear, fluid mental state. While strong emotions take will and strength to calm, changing your thoughts takes persistence. Breathe in Solar Light. Watch the flow of your thoughts as they float through your mind. If there are any thoughts you want to release, picture them leaving on your outbreath. Let all old, limited, or dense thoughts be carried away as you breathe out.

If any persistent thoughts continue to come into your mind, draw Solar Light into them with your inbreath. Surround each thought with so much Solar Light that it turns into light. Send these thoughts, transformed into light, out to the world with your outbreath. You can stay calm and peaceful no matter what thoughts you have. You can let thoughts come into your mind and turn them into light. Your mind can become clear as a mountain lake that reflects the sun and the sky above it like a mirror.

*Expand your consciousness with Solar Light to journey to the soul plane.*

Focus on the Solar Light above you. Let it draw you upward into a world of incredible, beautiful light, the light of the soul plane. As you look, you see sparkling, moving points of light everywhere. It appears that you are in a sea of light. Your consciousness is expanded; it is fluid light. You can travel anywhere, moving from point of light to point of light. You can become the space between the lights and move underneath them. You can roll, you can dance, you can bounce. You can spread out into infinity in the blink of an eye and contract into a small dot of light in the same blink. You can be at every point in the sea of light simultaneously. You can be a point of light floating in this sea, and you can be the sea itself. This is the soul plane of infinity, of light, of unlimited space, of no time. It is here that you can have the clearest sense of your soul because of the amplification of soul energy that is present.

The world of the soul plane does not know sorrow or pain. It knows only love, joy, and bliss. Currents of Solar Light flow outward and downward from the soul plane to the earth plane. As the energy moves downward, it also flows back upward, carrying all life below it back home. Think of the Solar Light shining upon you while you are in the soul plane. Receive its warm rays of light into your being. Feel its welcome, its love, and its joy. This is the light of transformation at every level.

*Picture yourself becoming
a more beautiful and perfect light.*

Hold the image of the Solar Light in your awareness until you have a stronger sense of it. As you observe the Solar Light, discover how it is continually becoming a more beautiful and perfect light. As you observe it, picture that you, too, are becoming a more beautiful and perfect light. Your inner light is becoming clearer, becoming more balanced, harmonious, and radiant. Each moment you bask in Solar Light, you are fulfilling one of your soul's purposes: to become a more beautiful and perfect light.

By working with the Solar Light, you can create profound changes in your life, your consciousness, and your spiritual path. The Solar Light is one of the most powerful forces in the universe. Think of the Solar Light as often as possible when you wake up or fall asleep, and at other times during the day. Doing this increases your ability to be aware of light and to radiate light. You can create many wonderful changes in your life in this way.

# Soul Play

Connect with the Solar Light in one or more of the following ways to expand your consciousness, preparing you to journey to the soul plane, where you will meet and blend with your soul.

1. Greet the Solar Light today as a living, loving Being. Receive a special ray of light from it directly into your heart center to awaken it.

2. Call Solar Light to you and create a cocoon of Solar Light all around you. Surround yourself in Solar Light all day.

3. When sunlight touches your body today, sense the particles of Solar Light contained within it. Imagine that these particles of Solar Light are evolving your body.

4. Breathe in Solar Light, and with your outbreath, send it to the DNA in the center of every cell in your body. Imagine you are evolving the code of life within you to take you to your next level of evolution.

5. Breathe in Solar Light to calm your emotions. With your outbreath, send Solar Light to any turbulent, negative, or intense emotions. Continue until you feel calmer.

6. Surround thoughts that you do not want with Solar Light until they turn into light. Be persistent and do this every time you experience these thoughts, until they no longer exist except as light.

7. Observe the Solar Light as it continually becomes a more beautiful and perfect light. Discover how you, too, are becoming a more beautiful and perfect light.

# Chapter 3

# Meeting Your Soul

*At the Temple of the Enlightened Ones in the soul plane,*
*you call your soul and it comes.*
*Your soul reveals its luminous light of Spirit*
*as you travel into your soul's jewel.*

It is time to meet your soul. To begin, find a physically comfortable position, one that allows you to relax. Think of the Solar Light and imagine its warm rays shining upon you. Take a deep breath in, breathing in Solar Light. Picture Solar Light flowing through your body, relaxing everywhere it touches. Draw in Solar Light until a cocoon of Solar Light forms around you. Add Solar Light to your emotions to calm them. Breathe Solar Light into your thoughts, and imagine old, limited thoughts leaving on your outbreath. Let your mind become quiet and clear. Feel the rays of Solar Light upon you, drawing you upward to the soul plane until you are in the sea of light. Play for a moment in the soul plane.

There is a place in the soul plane I will call the Temple of the Enlightened Ones, or simply the Temple. It is a place where Enlightened Ones such as the Masters and Beings of Light work for the good of humanity. They assist humanity in many ways, such as by broadcasting love, joy, harmony, peace, and hope. You will meet your soul here first, for the assistance available here can make soul contact easier.

Although you might imagine this Temple having walls and rooms, in reality it is composed of light and has no form. The Beings here are making it possible for you to see or sense it as forms and shapes. It may appear different each time you come to it, for it is composed of constantly changing patterns of light. You may not even experience it as a place; you may simply find it as light or recognize it by the feelings of love and inner peace you have as you think of it.

You are invited to come to this Temple. In the soul plane you can travel anywhere by making a picture of where you want to be. Go to the Temple by thinking of and having the intent to go to this high, beautiful place. Observe what the Temple looks or feels like as you approach it. You might picture, feel, or imagine the presence of the highest of Beings whose hearts are filled with pure love. You can be calm and peaceful here, happy and free. You are safe and loved in this wonderful place.

*Meet the souls of others who have*
*come to awaken their heart centers.*

At the Temple, a Being of Light meets you and leads you inside to the middle of an enormous courtyard. Look around and notice the souls of others who are here, preparing to make soul contact as you are. You will work with them often throughout this book. Some are the souls of friends and loved ones you know, or the souls of those you will meet in the future. Many are people who are reading this book as you are. Some are souls of those you may never meet in person, and you will join with them only on the soul plane. In addition, you are seeding many new wonderful friendships with people you *will* meet in this lifetime. You will recognize these people when you meet them by the wonderful feelings between you. Many will be friends with common interests who are on a path similar to yours. There is much power available to each person in joining together and playing as a group with others who are taking the same step. Send your love to those who are here. Observe the beautiful patterns of light you can make together as you play here.

## *J*oin the Beings of Light
### *who are here to assist you.*

The ceremony of meeting your soul is beginning. Because this ceremony takes place in the soul plane of no time, you can join at any time, and you will be entering just as it is occurring. The power of group members to call upon and meet their souls grows with each person who joins.

The Enlightened Ones have sent a call to request the presence of the Beings of Light whose purpose is to assist people in meeting their souls. As you watch, row upon row, tier upon tier of these Beings come to join you until you are surrounded by their beautiful light. They assist by amplifying your call to your soul. They have volunteered to work with you and will always be available whenever you request their assistance. In addition, many other Beings of Light have come to join you. Feel their love for you, their joy in being able to assist you during this important time. If you would like their assistance in calling your soul to you, ask them now.

It is time to call your soul to you. This is an important time for your soul. Your soul has been waiting for you to reach this stage of consciously connecting with it. As you connect with your soul, you give it the power and energy it needs to reach its next level of evolution. It has been in deep meditation, focusing its attention on the higher realms, waiting for you to become more aware of it. Once you contact your soul, more of your soul's energy will be focused upon you.

*Sound the note that
calls your soul to you.*

You can call your soul to you by sounding an inner note. There is a part of you that knows exactly how to do this. You have sounded this note before in those times when you called out for greater strength, wisdom, love, or assistance. Your soul came to you in those moments and blended its light with yours to increase your inner knowingness, strength, and courage. Now you are consciously calling it to you. You are requesting that your soul become a permanent part of your consciousness and establish more of its presence in your daily life.

Find the note you can sound from deep within you that calls your soul. This note carries the sound of your intention and says to your soul, "I am ready." This note may be a feeling, a tone, or a sound. Sound this note inwardly or make a sound aloud. Practice with an "om" or other sounds. There is no right or wrong way to call your soul, so do not worry if you have the right note or sound. The Beings of Light are assisting you in amplifying your call to your soul. Your soul will know your intention to meet it. It will hear your call and come.

When your soul hears your call, it responds by becoming visible to you. Watch as it approaches you. It may seem to come from far away, moving toward you until it is in front of you. Acknowledge the power of this moment. Feel the rush of energy and the sense of contact as your soul turns its attention onto you. It is delighted you have called it and are ready to link with it.

Discover how powerful, magnificent, and beautiful your soul is. Feel its vastness and its love. This is part of you! Your soul is an exquisite, wonderful, and divine being. It has so much love for you. Send your love to it, and open to receive its love for you.

*Greet your soul as a living presence
of great love, wisdom, and
intelligence.*

Observe anything you can about your soul. Notice any
patterns of light or colors within it. Whatever you can sense
about your soul is perfect, even if it feels as if you are making
it up. Or, you may not feel or see anything. Your soul can work
with you whether or not you are aware of it.

Picture your soul as an enormous, radiant sphere of light.
In its center is a beautiful, magnificent light that is veiled by
petals. There are twelve petals in four rows of three petals each.
They are not truly petals but vortexes of energy that surround
and veil this magnificent light. The central light in the middle
of your soul is like a luminous jewel. It is the source of your
soul's life, its source, its Spirit. As your soul evolves, these
petals come to reflect all the colors of the rainbow. When you
reach a certain stage of spiritual development, the petals unfold
completely, and this magnificent light becomes fully visible.

Now that you have called your soul, it is going to allow
you to move your awareness into its jewel. Your soul is making
its petals more transparent, revealing a magnificent, beautiful,
and luminous light, dazzling in its effect. Observe this jewel
in your soul's center with your inner eyes. Watch as light and
energy radiate from it. Initially you may only catch glimpses
of this light. Each time you think of it, you may notice that
you can see, sense, or feel more about it.

You might imagine yourself as very small, viewing an enormous light. You can send your awareness deeper and deeper
into your soul's jewel, moving into it with your mind. There
is no end to this light, for you are traveling into infinity. You
are merging with Source, with Spirit. As you travel into your
soul's jewel, you may find yourself expanding into a higher

state of consciousness. You may feel suspended inside an infinite world that is beyond time and space.

*Move your awareness*
*into your soul's jewel*
*to transform your consciousness.*

When your awareness is fully inside your soul's jewel, you may experience a stillness so profound you can only hold onto it for a moment. Bathe in the stillness of this luminous light. Let it flow through you. This light of Spirit has the power to transform you at every level. As you observe this luminous light in the center of your soul, it brings clarity of mind. It connects you with the very essence of your being. Become one with your soul's jewel as often as you would like. Every moment you think of it, feel it, or sense it, you are transforming your consciousness.

You have met your soul and harmonized with the light of Spirit. Your soul will work with you more actively as you begin to work more actively with it. Finish by thanking all the Beings of Light who have assisted you. Anytime you need assistance in calling your soul, you can ask the Beings of Light to assist you, and they will.

# Soul Play

From the list below, pick something to practice today with a sense of play to continue to expand your ability to meet and sense your soul.

1. Explore and discover more about the Temple of the Enlightened Ones. Go here at least once and absorb the feelings of peace, love, and joy that are present.

2. Join again with the souls of those you met at the Temple. Sense their delight in your being here. Receive their warm greetings. Send love to them and receive love back. Feel the love and light that are available when you join a group in this way. Working together as a group enhances everyone's ability to make soul contact.

3. Practice calling your soul to you. Sound an inner note or an "om" out loud. Ask the Beings of Light to amplify your call. Gain more confidence in your ability to call your soul to you and to have it respond.

4. Call your soul to you and greet it as a living, loving being. Open to receive its love for you. Send it your love.

5. Meet your soul and notice or sense anything you can about it. Observe its light, sense its presence, and feel the love it radiates.

6. Sense your soul's magnificent jewel. Go inside this jewel with your imagination, feeling the peace and stillness here. Let stillness permeate your being.

7. Travel into your soul's jewel and draw energy from it. Recharge yourself as you connect with Spirit, the essence of your being.

# Chapter 4

# Blending With Your Soul

*Your soul sends its light, love,
and will into your personality.
You know yourself as your soul.*

You have met your soul and are ready to take your next step
of blending with your soul. Find a comfortable position, one
that allows you to feel relaxed. Think of the Solar Light and
call it to you, surrounding your body in a cocoon of Solar
Light. Breathe in Solar Light and quiet your emotions. Add
Solar Light to your thoughts and watch them turn into light.
Breathe out Solar Light, and let all old, dense, or less expansive
thoughts flow out on your breath to be carried away. Your
mind is growing quiet and serene. Let yourself rise easily to
the soul plane, until you are in the sea of light with the
beautiful Solar Light shining upon you.

Think of the Temple of the Enlightened Ones until you
sense you are there. It may or may not appear the same as
the last time you came. Feel the peace and love all about you.
Notice the gentle breeze as it touches you. See the beauty all
around you. Smell the fragrance of the flowers. Make the image
of the Temple as real as you can.

Your presence is expected. You are met by a Being of Light
who leads you inside to the middle of the courtyard you were
in before. A ceremony of joining with your soul has been

planned for you and all the others who are preparing to blend with their souls. Greet the others who are here. Feel their love for and acceptance of you. Acknowledge the unity and the common purpose that all of you share as you prepare to blend with your souls.

Many Beings of Light have come to assist you. As you watch, row upon row and tier upon tier of Beings of Light are coming from the higher realms of light. Again the atmosphere becomes one of radiant, shimmering light. The Solar Light is overhead, shining its light on all. The Beings who can assist you in calling your soul have returned. In addition, there is another group of Beings of Light here to assist your personality in blending with your soul. You can call upon them anytime you feel you are resisting your soul, or when you want to blend with your soul and increase your awareness of its presence.

It is time to connect with your soul. Call your soul to you by sounding your soul's note. You can ask the Beings of Light to assist you in amplifying your call. Quiet your thoughts, take a deep breath in, and send out the note that calls your soul to you.

*Feel your soul's presence*
*like the touch*
*of an angel.*

Your soul hears you and draws nearer. Picture or imagine its radiant light coming toward you until it is directly in front of you. Sense its peaceful, loving presence. Feel its welcome to you, its gentle acceptance of and love for you. It is so joyful that you want to blend with it. As your soul prepares to merge with you, it asks you again, "Are you ready to blend with me?" Make sure you are ready before you take this next step. Although your soul has always been a part of you, it has not blended with you in this way before. Your soul's energy is so powerful that it will change your life as it adds its energy to yours. If you do not feel ready, work with your subpersonalities until you can answer, "Yes, I am ready."

When you are ready, your soul approaches. It slowly and respectfully begins to surround you. Let the sphere of light of your soul gently enfold your body with its jewel of light around your heart center. You might take a moment to close your eyes and experience this blending as fully as you can. Feel yourself encompassed in light. Picture moving patterns of light all around you. Find one pattern of light and let yourself "fall" into it. Feel yourself becoming the light of your soul as you do, for your soul is composed of light.

*Let your soul's*
*higher frequency light*
*blend with the light*
*of your personality.*

With each breath, draw your soul closer to you and open to receive its light. Picture the light of your soul blending with the light of your personality. At first there may be some friction, for the light of your personality and the light of your soul each have a different frequency. As the blending proceeds, you become radiant with soul light. Call upon the Beings of Light who assist the personality in blending with the soul to make this a smooth, easy blending for you and your soul.

As more of your soul's light flows into you, feel its power. Let currents of its light and power flow through you. Before you continue, take a moment to feel the power of your soul as it flows through you. Open to receive from your soul the energy that would most assist you in reaching a new level of light.

*Sense your soul
lighting the way for you.*

Feel your soul's light and energy pulsing through you. Imagine that its light is so great that it always lights a path in front of you for you to see and follow. It shows you the light that is all about you, in yourself and in others. Sense your soul's light, lighting up your highest path and creating light all about you. Receive your soul's light into your mind. Let your soul bring you new thoughts, ideas, and creative inspiration.

Your soul purifies all it touches. As your soul bathes you in its light of purification, it transforms lower energies within you into their higher expressions. Experience the transformative power of your soul as its purifying light moves through you. Draw your soul's light into every cell and atom in your body. Imagine a tiny light in the center of each cell and atom growing radiant with the luminous light of your soul.

Allow the love of your soul to flow through you so you can know and express its love. Feel the essence of soul love pouring through your heart center. You are absorbing your soul's love and expanding your ability to love. Feel your soul's emotions of joy and bliss, of peace and serenity.

Your soul is unlimited and knows no boundaries. It is creative and intelligent. Your soul can take you far beyond what you think is possible in your life. It can lift you into the higher realms, expanding your capacity to think and to create. Take a moment to draw in your soul's energy of expansion so you can release limits and claim your unlimited potential.

Your soul is aligned with the Higher Will. It knows the higher purpose of your life. You can absorb this knowledge every time you blend with your soul. Ask for your soul's will to flow through you, showing you more of the higher purpose of your life.

*Look at yourself
through your soul's eyes.
See the beauty of your being.*

Let your awareness expand into your soul's consciousness, as if you are becoming your soul. You might imagine yourself growing larger as your awareness spreads out into your soul's "body." Expand into your soul's consciousness until you can sense life from your soul's perspective. You may not feel anything different. Or, you may become aware of subtle changes. As your soul, look at yourself and your life. Your soul always sees beauty, perfection, and love. Acknowledge how beautiful you are as you look at yourself through your soul's eyes.

You have done it! You have blended with your soul. Whether or not you sensed this union, your soul has begun to join and work with you in new and wonderful ways. Thank the Beings of Light for all the gifts you have received from them and for their assistance.

You may want to repeat these steps several more times to get a clearer sense of what it feels like to become your soul. Much more has happened than you may realize. You have planted many seeds. Many wonderful changes can now occur. They may be subtle at first, yet they will come into your life.

# Soul Play

Pick one soul quality to experience from the list below. Let the quality you pick flow through you as you blend with your soul.

- **Presence.** If you feel lonely, tired, stressed, or if you feel you do not have enough strength to do all you need to do, blend with your soul and be aware of its healing, loving presence.
- **Love.** If you have a critical thought about yourself or others, or if you want to feel more love and compassion, ask your soul to fill you with its love.
- **Light.** When you need to have your highest path or choices become more visible, or to sense the light in a situation, call upon your soul's light to illuminate the way for you.
- **Purity.** If you want to let go of old forms, release lower energies, or raise your vibration, open and receive your soul's purifying and cleansing energy.
- **Expansion.** When you want to expand your mind, lift your emotions, or open to new ideas, let your soul's expansiveness flow through you.
- **Will.** Before you make an important decision, or guide or counsel others, allow your soul's will to flow through you, aligning you with the Higher Will.
- **Joy.** Whenever you are feeling burdened, tired, depressed, or overwhelmed, stop and blend with your soul. Let its joy flow through you. Sound your soul's note of joy as you move through the day.

# Chapter 5

# Living as Your Soul

*The power, love, light, will, and presence of your soul
become a part of your daily life.*

You have blended with your soul and felt its presence. You
now have access to more of the unlimited power, love, and
light of your soul. Your most powerful experiences of your soul
may initially come when you contact your soul in a state of
meditation. Once you have done this, you can learn to call
upon it during ordinary moments, sense its presence, and
make it a part of your daily life. With practice, you can call
your soul to you, blend with it, and experience its presence
just by thinking of it. Blending with your soul throughout the
day will greatly enhance your ability to live as your soul.
Working with your soul is an important step to take on your
journey of enlightenment.

Connect with your soul without going to the soul plane
by breathing calmly and evenly a few times. Picture the Solar
Light and fill yourself with its light. Let it assist you in calming
your emotions and clearing your mind. Think of your soul and
call it to you. Sense your soul surrounding your body as you
blend with it. Stop reading for a moment, and practice calling
your soul to you and blending with it until you can imagine
or sense its presence.

Some of you will find it easy to recognize when your soul is present, since you have prior experience in sensing subtle energies. Some of you are just starting on a path of spiritual growth, or have less experience with meditation or with sensing subtle energies. You may need to practice blending with your soul more often before you can experience your soul's presence. Even if you have no awareness of your soul's presence, continue calling it to you and blending with it. You do not need to be able to feel, see, or hear your soul to experience the benefits of soul contact.

You may find that your ability to sense your soul varies from time to time. You might have distinct feelings when you connect with your soul one time, and no feelings the next. Some people have a powerful initial experience of their soul, then find soul contact less dramatic the next few times. After you have worked with your soul, its presence may feel so familiar that you no longer experience it dramatically. Your sense of your soul may depend on the state you are in when you blend with it. For instance, if you start from a calm, flowing emotional state, it may be easier to feel your soul's peace and serenity. Most of you will have a growing ability to sense your soul as you blend with it in a variety of circumstances and over a period of time.

*Observe your experience of your soul
in various environments.*

The following are suggestions of when to call upon and experience your soul. Connect with your soul in various situations to learn more about your soul and how its presence can change your life for the better. Make soul contact often so that your soul's presence, power, light, love, will, and other qualities can become more a part of your daily life.

Draw your soul to you and feel its presence flow through you while you are in various environments. Blend with your soul when you are in a garden with flowers, in nature, at home, with friends, in a crowd, in public places, or in a spiritual place. Link with your soul when you are sitting in sunlight. Explore how your perception of and ability to sense your soul can change when you are in different environments and circumstances.

Merge with your soul when you are in various moods. Connect with it when you are feeling good and peaceful, and when you are feeling confused, tired, fearful, or highly emotional. Notice if there is even a slight change in how you feel. Good feelings may become amplified, and distressing emotions may become more flowing and peaceful.

*Notice your experience of your soul
around different people.*

Pay attention to your ability to be aware of your soul around children, family, friends, business associates, casual acquaintances, and strangers. Connect with your soul when you are with a spiritual leader. Notice if your experience of your soul changes depending upon whom you are with. Explore if your experience of people changes after you blend with your soul. You might find yourself opening your heart and expressing love in new ways. Perhaps you can respond with love instead of being defensive or fearful. Or, the topic of conversation or the energy between you may change in some positive way. You may experience your perspective changing from a focus on yourself and your life to an increasing awareness of how your actions affect others. You may find yourself feeling more compassionate and concerned about others. You may be more willing to listen and have less attachment to getting your way, choosing peace over conflict. You may choose to love with a wise, mature love that serves people's souls rather than catering to the whims of their personalities.

Think of your soul and blend with it during various activities. Connect with your soul when you meditate. Join with it during ordinary activities, such as when you are doing housework, driving, reading, writing, playing games, or watching television. Notice what changes. Link with your soul when you are standing, sitting, exercising, or lying down. Have fun! Be playful and inventive as you think of ways to experience and know your soul. Make your soul a part of your daily life, not something you connect with only during special occasions.

What follows are some experiences you may have as you blend with your soul. You may or may not have any of the experiences described. Let whatever experiences you have be the perfect ones for you. There are as many different ways to know your soul as there are people.

## *Feel your soul's confidence, courage, and joy.*

When you join with your soul you may experience many positive feelings about yourself. You may feel more peaceful, confident, and courageous. When you call upon your soul in difficult situations, its power and presence can change the way you feel about yourself and the circumstances in your life.

Blending with your soul may increase your sense of size. Your awareness may change from sensing yourself as the size of your body to feeling larger than your physical body. You might be aware of your soul as around and inside your body, or outside your body, or both. However you experience your soul is fine. Explore if your body feels different or if you have any new physical sensations. Some people feel sleepy when blending with their souls, while others feel very alert.

When you connect with your soul you may experience subtle qualities of light. You might sense or imagine a golden light, a white light, a multicolored light, or simply increased light all about you. Your soul may appear to your inner eyes as shimmering light; as glowing, luminous light; as steady, bright light; or as many other qualities of light. You may note greater light around you or feelings of more openness and love. When you blend with your soul you may feel as if you have become an enormous light or an angel of light.

As you meet and blend with your soul, you might feel as if you are reuniting with a dearly loved friend or family member who has been gone for a long time. You might feel a sense of "coming home," as if being with your soul is something you have experienced before.

You might experience your soul in subtle ways you cannot describe or put into words, although you have a sense that something is different. Use your imagination to know your soul. Your imagination is a very important tool that assists you in knowing your soul. Your imagination is both a creative force that works upon subtle energies to create changes in them, and a way to sense subtle energies.

Think of your soul often. Practice viewing your life from your soul's perspective, even if it seems as if you are making things up. Joining with your soul can change your perspective on your problems. Your priorities can change. What seems important to your personality may seem insignificant when your soul is present. You may think about things in a different way, or have new insights and understandings. Join with your soul when you are planning or thinking about your future. Discover any changes in your thoughts or perspectives about the issues you are thinking of. Note any expansion in your thinking. Pay attention to new creative ideas that may appear.

*A*sk *your soul, "What are your*
*purposes and goals for today?"*

To live as your soul is to start imagining that you *are* your soul. Wonder and ask yourself, "What would I, as my soul, do in this area of my life? What action could I take that would reflect my soul's purposes and goals?" Mentally ask your soul, "How can I open to receive more of your energy and love? How can I serve you in accomplishing your goals? How might I work with you more effectively?" Although you may not receive specific answers, simply asking these questions draws information into your mind that will emerge later as new insights and understandings.

If you find yourself forgetting to blend with your soul, or if you think of it yet resist making soul contact, continue working with your subpersonalities. Perhaps you have a sub-personality who feels it will not be needed if your soul does everything. It may feel that it can do everything itself and does not need your soul. Your subpersonalities need to be included in your journey to live as your soul. This is a cooperative venture between your personality, with all its subpersonalities, and your soul—you reaching upward and your soul reaching downward. As you evolve your subpersonalities, they can make the journey with you, growing and expanding until they, too, are transformed.

*R*eceive *your soul's love for you.*

Pause for a moment and open to receive love from your soul. As you accept your soul's love, say to yourself, "I deserve love. I now allow unlimited love into my life." As you accept love from your soul you develop the ability to receive.

Your growing ability to receive love can allow you to embrace all the gifts the universe and your soul have to offer you. Notice and appreciate all the good things you already have. Gratitude draws even more good things to you from your soul and the universe.

Open to receive your soul's love as often as you can remember. Your soul knows you are a magnificent and wonderful being. It loves your humanness and your divinity. It is incapable of judging you, of being mad at, disappointed in, or angry with you. It celebrates every time you love yourself, knowing that as you love and honor yourself, you grow closer to it. Your soul loves and accepts you, with no exceptions!

# Soul Play

Deepen and strengthen your experience of your soul in one or more of the following ways:

1. Practice blending with your soul several times today, paying attention to any subtle sensations that help you to know your soul is present.

2. Blend with your soul when you are in a calm emotional state, and when you are not. Observe how your emotional state changes your experience of your soul. Note how blending with your soul changes your emotional state.

3. Pick a new environment in which to blend with your soul. Discover what changes as you experience your soul in different environments.

4. At least once today, stop before you take action, blend with your soul, and ask, "What would I, as my soul, do in this situation?"

5. Open to receive your soul's love for you. Say to yourself, "I deserve love. I now allow unlimited love into my life."

6. Increase your ability to receive by expressing gratitude for all the gifts you have already received from your soul and the universe.

7. If for any reason you are resisting blending with your soul, identify and work with any resistant subpersonalities. In addition, ask the Beings of Light to assist you in blending with your soul.

# Section II

# Awakening Your Heart Centers

*You blend your heart center's jewel*
*with your soul's jewel.*
*Light from your heart center*
*moves up to your head center.*
*You know the serenity*
*and oneness of love.*
*Your soul activates*
*a hidden point of light*
*in your solar plexus center.*
*You know your soul's will to love.*
*You raise solar plexus energy*
*into your heart center*
*and surrender to love.*
*Light circulates among your heart centers.*
*You love as your soul.*

# Chapter 6

# Preparing to Awaken

*You prepare to awaken your heart centers
through learning more about them
and how they are awakened.*

Now that you have made soul contact, you can join with your soul to awaken your heart centers. You are taking an important step on your path to enlightenment as you do. As you learn to love, your soul can give you many of its other gifts, for you can be trusted to use them to create good things for yourself and others. With awakened heart centers, you can receive the love of the Enlightened Ones who broadcast love to humanity. You can become a source of love and attract to yourself many opportunities to make a difference in the world.

There are three heart centers you will work with in this book to increase your ability to embody soul love. As I have already mentioned in the Introduction, the first is located in an area around your physical heart. I call this your *primary heart center* or *heart center* (singular). The second is the heart of your head center, located in an area near the middle of the top of your head. I call this your *head center*. The third is your *solar plexus center*, located in an area around your navel. Your heart, head, and solar plexus are the three centers I call your *heart centers*. Refer to the illustration of your three heart centers on page 44. When these three centers are awakened and soul energy circulates among them, you can experience soul love.

You have seven major centers, including the three heart centers you will work with in this book. People also call these *chakras, subtle energy centers,* and *wheels of life.* These centers are not located in your physical body. They exist as subtle energies in what I will call your aura or etheric body. These seven centers begin with the first center at the base of your spine, and ascend to your head center (also known as your crown chakra) at the top of your head.

These seven centers have many functions. They are composed of streams of energy that come from your soul. They act as receivers and transmitters of your soul's energy. Some give life and vitality to your physical body. Other centers develop your higher consciousness.

There are three centers below your diaphragm. The three lower centers, including your solar plexus center, interact with energies in the three-dimensional world of form and matter. They are called the lower centers because they primarily affect your physical life, such as how you manifest, your personality, and your relationship to the world and the people around you. Your heart center is in between your higher and lower centers, and energy from above and below passes through it. Above your heart center are three higher centers, including your head center. These three higher centers primarily influence your intellectual and spiritual life.

There are many systems that define the functions of each center. Often different qualities, functions, and states of consciousness are assigned to the same centers depending on which system you study. There is no one right way to classify the functions of the centers. The subject of the centers and their functions is vast and complex. The qualities I have chosen to emphasize are those that awaken your heart centers. You may discover other systems defining the functions of each center differently than I have described them in this book. If so, discover what is useful to you about that system and use it to better understand yourself.

## *B*lend with your soul
## to awaken your heart centers.

There are many ways to awaken your heart centers. They are continuously evolving through your acts of love, thoughts of compassion, and your choice to feel your oneness with others. You awaken your heart centers by expressing soul love through inclusiveness, forgiveness, and unconditional love. Group work, love of humanity, and serving are powerful ways to awaken your heart centers. The way you live your daily life, relate to people, speak, act, and live gradually and definitely awakens your heart centers.

You can also awaken your heart centers by linking with your soul and practicing the qualities of soul love that awaken each center. You can learn to connect your heart centers through circulating energy among them to assist you in experiencing and expressing soul love.

In the chapters that follow, you will learn how to blend with your soul to awaken your three heart centers. The processes you will learn to direct energy from one center to another are symbolic representations of how to work with your centers. As you play with these images you can awaken your centers through your intent to do so. Use the images I have given, or be creative and let your soul guide you to the images that are most appropriate for you. There is no right or wrong way to awaken your centers. Besides picturing them, feel or sense them. Trust that however you choose to work with your heart centers is the right way for you.

It is fine if you cannot visualize or make a mental picture of your centers. Picturing, sensing, or imagining your heart centers is not necessary to awaken them. Your intent to work with them and to express love will naturally evolve your centers. Check each step with your soul before you take it, and proceed when you sense the rightness of doing so. Always follow your inner guidance if it differs from my instructions. Make yourself and your soul the authority on what is right for you.

In addition to learning how to direct energy among your centers, you will learn qualities of soul love to practice to awaken your heart centers. Each quality, such as magnetism or transparency, contains elements of all the other qualities of soul love. This is because all the qualities have the same essence—the essence of soul love. I have assigned certain soul-love qualities to specific centers. You might think of each heart center as a part of a holograph of your soul. Each center contains within it the complete energies of your soul and all its qualities. However, some centers provide easier doorways than others to experience certain soul qualities. I have chosen soul-love qualities to practice with each center that are most easily felt and experienced from that center. However, the goal is to be able to experience all the qualities of soul love as an integrated whole—the experience of soul love.

As you radiate soul love you may feel a shift in yourself. Some of you will feel this shift as an "aha," a release, or a feeling of greater love. You may feel a physical sensation of some sort, such as a lessening of tension somewhere in your body. You may discern a change in your attitude. All of these are indications that your heart centers are awakening.

As you practice the soul-love qualities, you may or may not note any immediate differences in your ability to be more consistently loving. Changes usually happen in subtle and gradual ways. Rapid growth is not necessary; what is important is to grow at a pace that is right for you. You do not need to be perfect and loving all the time to awaken your heart centers.

Every moment of feeling and expressing love brings you closer to your soul and awakens your heart centers. Even working with each quality once as you read will add to the radiance of your heart center and further awaken it.

As your heart centers awaken, issues of the heart may arise, including denied or buried pain. If you find your lessons coming too fast, or your awakening too rapid, stop focusing on awakening your heart centers for a while. Open to receive your soul's love for you during these times, calling upon your soul to assist you in releasing the past and opening to love.

Practice all the soul-love qualities with a sense of adventure, discovery, and exploration. There is not one "right" way to practice soul love. Let go of any judgment, and do not worry about following my instructions "correctly." Your soul has a marvelous capacity for joy and play. Make your experiences of expressing soul love fun and playful. Let them bring out the child within you that loves to explore and try new things. Be creative and use your imagination. Discover for yourself more of the qualities and expressions of soul love that are possible as you connect with your soul and express soul love.

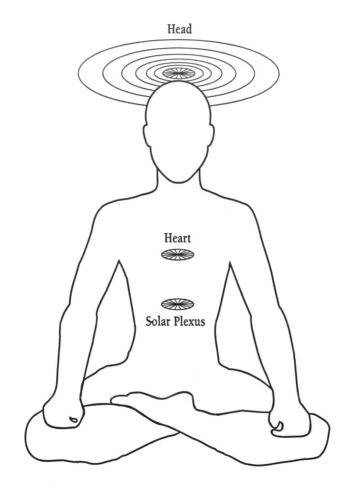

*Location of Three Heart Centers*

# CHAPTER 7

# Awakening Your Heart Center

*The Being of Love joins you
as you align your heart center's jewel
with your soul's jewel.*

You are ready to blend with your soul in a special way that will assist you in awakening your heart center. Start by journeying to the soul plane. Call Solar Light to yourself and surround your body in a cocoon of its light. Breathe in Solar Light and allow your emotions to become quiet and serene. Add Solar Light to your thoughts and watch them turn into light. Breathe out Solar Light, and let all old, dense, or less expansive thoughts flow out on your breath to be carried away. Expand your consciousness with Solar Light and travel to the soul plane until you are at the Temple of the Enlightened Ones.

At the Temple, a Being of Light meets you and leads you inside to the middle of a courtyard. Many Beings of Light are here, including those who assisted you in calling and blending with your soul. A ceremony of awakening your primary heart center is beginning.

Look around with your inner eyes, and greet all the others who are arriving to awaken their heart centers as you are. Feel the love that is present and the beauty of the light that all of you are forming as you join together. Send everyone your blessings.

The Beings of Light ask all of you here to form a circle, leaving an open space in the middle. A profound silence comes over everyone present as a Great Being makes an appearance in the center of the circle. This Being descends from a higher realm, first appearing as a shimmering light, then taking on more substance as he or she comes more fully into view. This Being is not truly male or female, for this Being has merged its male and female aspects. However, this Being may take on a specific appearance to assist you in knowing and recognizing its presence.

## Welcome the Being of Love
### into your life.

Feel, sense, or imagine the presence of this very great Being who has joined your group. The light coming from this Being is enormous. This Being has reached enlightenment and possesses fully awakened heart centers. This Being is here to sponsor you in making soul contact and in awakening your heart centers. For the rest of this book, I will refer to this great presence as the Being of Love.

There are several Beings of Love, including those called the Lords of Love, the Masters of Compassion, the Angels of Divine Love, Goddesses, and others whom I have not named. Whichever Being of Love appears to you will depend upon who you are and which Being is sponsoring you. These Beings have great love for humanity. They have chosen the path of compassion. Those who select the path of compassion love humanity so much they stay to aid humanity even when they could ascend to a higher plane themselves. They will stay until all of humanity has reached liberation.

Sense the Being of Love who has come to work with you and to teach you more about soul love. This Being will be sponsoring you as you awaken your heart centers. This Being embodies the highest principles of love, and is a model for you of fully awakened heart centers. Loving you, teaching you, and assisting you in awakening your heart centers are part of this Being's purpose and joy.

If you are ever questioning how to express soul love, you can invite the Being of Love into your heart center to show you the most loving way to be. Take a moment to pause and greet this Being. Observe with your inner eyes anything you can about this Being. Note its radiant heart center and the light that radiates from this Being. Imagine this Being greeting you. Feel how special you are to this Being, and how much this Being loves you.

The Being of Love will radiate love to your heart center to prepare it to receive more of your soul's love. Before the Being of Love can send you energy, you need to ask to receive it. You might say something such as, "I request your transmission of love, and I open my heart to receive it."

After you make this statement, get quiet, close your eyes, and open to receive energy from the Being of Love. Receive the first transmission directly into your heart center. You might sense this transmission as vibration, light, love, or sound. However, you do not need to see, sense, or feel anything for this transmission to awaken your heart centers. As you receive the love and energy being sent to you, feel your heart center becoming more radiant with love.

Next, the Being sends you love that allows you to know that you are always safe, protected, and watched over wherever you may be. This is a broadcast of love that calls high Beings and angels to you who will be your "invisible" helpers to make sure you are always safe. Say to yourself, "I am always safe and protected wherever I am" as you receive this second broadcast of love.

## *Observe the beautiful jewel in your heart center.*

You are ready to join with your soul to awaken your heart center. You might sense your heart center as located around the area of your physical heart. (See illustration on page 44.) Like your soul, your heart center has a beautiful, exquisite central jewel surrounded by twelve petals, arranged in four rows of three petals each. Some petals are open, some are partly open, and some are closed like a rosebud. The jewel in the middle is hidden by the unopened petals. When your heart center is fully awakened, all its petals unfold and its central jewel shines out in its full beauty.

Your soul and the Being of Love will assist you in viewing this jewel of your heart center. As you look at it with your inner eyes, it is as if you are going to a sacred space within you. Imagine the jewel in the middle of your heart center as a many-faceted diamond with light pouring out from within it. All the colors of the rainbow shine out from the facets of this jewel. It is so beautiful that you feel more whole and complete just looking at it. Imagine this jewel revolving slowly, with sparkling, shimmering light coming out of it. Sense the essence of love flowing out through this diamond, each facet radiating a different quality of love.

Sound the note that calls your soul to you until you can sense its presence. Greet your soul and feel its gentleness, its caring, and its love for you. It is so glad that you have called upon it. You are going to blend with your soul in a special way that will aid you in awakening your heart center. The Being of Love is present to assist you. Watch as your soul comes closer to you until it is right above the top of your head. Gently and easily your soul descends, moving down through your head center to your heart center. Sense how lovingly and gently your soul blends with you.

## *Merge your heart center's jewel with your soul's jewel.*

Your soul descends to your heart center, until its jewel surrounds your heart center's jewel. Your soul's jewel is much larger than your heart center's jewel; your heart's jewel fits inside it. Your soul makes many fine adjustments until the jewel in your heart center is surrounded by and fully inside the jewel in your soul's center. There may be a special moment when there is a "click" or a shift as the two jewels move into alignment with each other. You may experience an almost physical feeling when this happens. With this alignment, your soul stimulates the potential of love within your heart center. Your heart center's jewel becomes brighter and more beautiful. The petals of your heart center respond by opening a bit more, so that the radiant light of your heart center's jewel is more fully revealed.

These two jewels exist in different dimensions. Your heart center's jewel begins to vibrate in harmony with your soul's jewel. You can almost hear the tone they are sending out if you listen with your inner ears. It is as if they are two beautiful crystals sounding their pure notes together. Their tones blend and become one, creating a symphony of sound so beautiful, powerful, and profound that it heals and soothes everything it touches. This tone sends love into the atoms and cells of your body. Its melody goes out into the universe, like a beacon of love, nurturing all it touches.

## *Invite the Being of Love into your heart center.*

You can invite the Being of Love into your heart center to aid you in expressing and embodying soul love. With the presence of this Being in your heart center, you can experience a constant refinement of your ability to radiate soul love and an ongoing awakening of your heart center. To bring this Being into your heart center, picture yourself as very small. Observe your heart center's jewel as if it were an enormous, radiant jewel of light in front of you. Invite the Being of Love into the middle of your heart center's jewel. Feel the Being of Love enter into your heart center. You might imagine a very small image of the Being of Love standing in the middle of your heart center's jewel. Your heart center grows even more beautiful and radiant with love. Observe all you can, then return to your normal size. You can invite the Being of Love into your heart center any time you want, or you can ask for the Being of Love to stay permanently in your heart center. Absorb this wonderful love and allow the Being of Love to assist you in awakening your heart center and expressing soul love.

*Travel into the light
of your heart center's jewel.*

Picture your heart center as the center of your being, your true self. This is the self that is wise, serene, forgiving, inclusive, and compassionate. The light coming from your heart center's jewel as it blends with your soul's jewel dissolves, transforms, and evolves those energies within you that do not reflect your true being. It releases worry, tension, fear, shadows of the past, and all other things that keep you from knowing your soul's love.

Your soul pours its life-force energy into you through your heart center. Picture soul love flowing from your heart center into your physical heart, and from there into your bloodstream. Imagine your soul's sparkling light moving through your bloodstream, circulating pure love throughout your body. This stream of love flows through your arteries and veins, cleansing, revitalizing, and rejuvenating you. Your soul is bringing its life force energy to every part of your body. Sense this as a spiritual flow of life, pure and perfect, moving through your body. Picture the circulation of love and energy moving freely, touching every part of you. As your soul vitalizes your heart center, you can feel more energy and aliveness.

Practice blending with your soul and aligning your heart center's jewel with your soul's jewel over and over. Become familiar with the subtle feelings and images that taking this step can create.

Thank the Being of Love who has joined you. Take a moment to sense this Being's heart center. Observe your heart center and imagine it becoming like the heart center of the Being of Love. Picture the petals of your heart center opening and the jewel in the middle becoming more visible. The jewel of your heart center and your soul's jewel are sounding a note of love together. Sense soul love flowing out from you to everyone you know.

# Soul Play

Pick from the list below one or more ways to awaken your heart center:

1. Journey to the Temple and view your heart center's jewel as a many-faceted diamond. As you look at it, imagine going to a sacred space within you. It is so beautiful that you feel more whole and complete just looking at it.

2. Receive a transmission from the Being of Love to awaken your heart center. Affirm as you receive this transmission that you are ready to express more love in your daily life.

3. Whenever you feel afraid, say to yourself, "I am always safe and protected." Feel the Being of Love call high Beings and angels to assist you.

4. Align your heart center's jewel with your soul's jewel. Practice this often, imagining a click or shift as they come together. Listen with your inner ears to the beautiful tone they create together.

5. Invite the Being of Love into your heart center whenever you want to feel or act more loving. Notice any changes in your ability to feel and express love.

6. Be aware of your heart center today as a radiant light that extends beyond your body, touching everyone around you with love.

7. If you are sick, tired, or simply want more energy, blend your heart center's jewel with your soul's jewel. Imagine soul love flowing from your heart center into your physical heart and then into your bloodstream, revitalizing and rejuvenating you.

# CHAPTER 8

# Soul Linking

*Light radiates from your heart center
to another person's heart center.
With the Solar Light above both of you,
a triangle of light is formed and a soul link is made.*

Soul linking is a way to awaken your heart centers and express soul love to others. It is an important skill, one that you can use to evolve your relationships. To soul link, you will be guided to make certain patterns of light with people. You can practice these patterns first in your mind, when other people are not physically present. With practice, you can make these patterns of light easily and automatically whenever you are with people. The soul-linking patterns of light and the images you use do not have to be exact. Play with the images presented, and use them in whatever way works for you. You may change them, enhance them, or create new images.

Soul linking is a way of radiating love to people. Radiating love may feel as if you are "sending" love to others. However, you are not really sending love. Reception happens instantaneously through the principle of resonance. You might have experienced this when you were around someone who was happy, and suddenly you chose to feel happier yourself. The other person did not send you happiness; instead you began to resonate with this person's vibration of happiness. The happiness you felt was not the other person's; it was your own. You could choose to experience happiness, or not. In the same way, when you soul link you are not sending energy to others. You are radiating various qualities of soul love because you feel them yourself. If others feel them, it is because they resonate with the qualities of love you are radiating and choose to feel them.

Close your eyes for a moment, and let an image of someone come into your mind to soul link with and radiate love to. You can soul link to evolve a relationship with someone special, or with someone you have not yet met, such as a soul mate. You can soul link with friends and loved ones, children, parents, relatives, and colleagues. You can soul link with people you knew in the past and those you will meet in the future. You can soul link to complete or continue a relationship with someone who has died or who is in a coma, for souls can link across time and space.

*Create a line of light between*
*your heart center*
*and another person's.*

Imagine that the person you have chosen is in front of you. Let your image of this person's body fade until you can picture this person's heart center as radiant light. Call your soul to you. Watch as your soul descends through your head center to your heart center. Observe as your heart center's jewel aligns with your soul's jewel. With this alignment, you might imagine sparkling, shimmering, diamondlike light radiating from your primary heart center. Picture a ray of light coming out from your heart center and touching the other person's heart center. You can use any image that feels right to you. Some people imagine a ray of light connecting their heart centers. Some perceive a cord, filament, or narrow or wide band of light, or shimmering rays of light flowing out from their heart center to another person's heart center. You may detect ray after ray of light coming from your heart center out to the other person's heart center, or a steady beam. You may simply sense that your heart center is becoming so bright that the light coming out from it touches the other person's heart center. What is important is a sense of a connection between your two heart centers.

I am using the image of a line of light as a symbol for a heart connection. Choose any picture or image that works for you to remind you to connect heart-to-heart when you are with other people. And, it is fine if you do not use any image. Just sensing or having the intention to make a heart connection is all that is important for this first step of soul linking.

## Connect with the other person's soul.

The second important element of soul linking is to become aware of your soul and other people's souls as you make a heart connection. As you do, you strengthen your connection to your own soul. You become aware that you have a soul connection to others that is even more important than your personality relationship with them. When you connect with other people's souls, it is easier to do those things that honor their souls instead of being influenced by their personality desires.

Make a heart connection once again with the person you just chose to radiate love to. Discover anything you can about how you sense the other person's soul. You may experience this person's soul in various ways. You may feel more love, compassion, or peace as you connect with this person's soul. You may have a stronger experience of your own soul. You may notice more light. Detect everything you can about your soul connection and how it is different from your personality connection. Allow your personality issues to drop away and appreciate the light and beauty of this person's soul. It is fine if you do not sense anything. The intention to connect with the other person's soul is all that is necessary for a soul connection to occur.

## *Picture the Solar Light above both of you.*

The final step of soul linking is to picture the Solar Light above both of you as you make a line of light between your heart centers. This brings the highest love and the light of oneness to your relationship. It connects both of you in higher purpose. It adds Solar Light to your interactions with each other, bringing more harmony, beauty, balance, and clarity to your relationship. Every moment you focus on Solar Light expands the potential for love between you. Thinking of the Solar Light above both of you as you soul link makes it easier to experience your soul and to radiate soul love.

Make a line of light between your heart center and the person you just connected with. Note the Solar Light above both of you. Watch as a ray of light comes down from the Solar Light, descending through your head center into your heart center, then moving out to the other person's heart center through your heart connection. Solar Light descends through the other person's head center to the heart center, and then out to your heart center.

You have formed a triangle of light between you and the other person. Solar Light is at the top of the triangle. The base of the triangle is the line of light between your heart centers. Solar Light is circulating through this triangle. When you make a line of light between your heart center and another person's heart center, sense your soul and the other person's soul, and bring the Solar Light into your connection, you are *soul linking*.

Although I have used the Solar Light as the higher light guiding your relationship, you may use any higher light that works for you. This could be a star, a high Being such as an angel, Being of Light, Master, God, the Goddess, the All-That-Is, and so on. What is most important is that you are aware of a light that is higher than both of your souls, guiding you as you make a soul connection. The Solar Light harmonizes, balances, lifts the energies between you, and draws your attention upward to the light. You may want to work first with the image of the Solar Light above both of you, and later try other types of light to guide your relationship as you soul link.

*I*nvite the Being of Love
*into your heart center*
*as you soul link.*

As you soul link, you can evolve your relationships by inviting the Being of Love into your heart center. You can ask for this Being to be present to assist you in feeling or acting more loving. The Being of Love can assist you if you are in difficult situations, or need strength or courage to love as your soul. Soul link with one of the people you have chosen. Make a line of light between your heart centers, connect with the other person's soul, and imagine the Solar Light above both of you. Invite the Being of Love into your heart center. Notice any changes as you do this. Imagine yourself loving, thinking, and acting as the Being of Love. Ask yourself, "How would I, as a Being of Love, express soul love to this person?" Let the Being of Love stimulate your ability to love with tenderness, wisdom, and compassion. You do what is loving and wise, not to comfort people's personality, but to empower them to grow and evolve spiritually.

$$Pay\ attention\ to\ your\ energy$$
$$to\ know\ if\ your\ love$$
$$is\ being\ received.$$

Now that you have practiced soul linking, you can learn a few energy principles of radiating love. This will prepare you for radiating the various qualities of soul love you will explore later. These principles teach you how energy works—how to know if others have chosen to resonate with your love, how to increase your radiance of love, and how to know when to stop radiating love.

Soul link with the person you have chosen. Picture a line of light between your heart centers. The Solar Light is above both of you. Sense your soul and the soul of the other person. Radiate love to the other person, a love that lifts, soothes, and comforts. You can know if the other person is receiving your love by observing yourself. Pay attention to your feelings, thoughts, and energy. If the other person is receiving the love you are radiating, you will feel more open, expansive, joyful, or loving as you soul link. You may find it easier to sense and contact your soul.

Do not rely on people's outer responses as your feedback about whether they have received your love. People may not respond in any outer way you can measure or observe. Or, they may respond by acting more loving, open, or different in some way. More important than other people's reactions is your increasing ability to experience your soul and to radiate soul love. You can know that the other person is resonating with the love you are radiating by your increasing joy and ease in doing it.

*Intensify your broadcast of love*
*when the love you radiate*
*is being received.*

If others are responding to the love you are radiating, you can intensify your broadcast of soul love in several ways. You can intensify your broadcast of love by feeling the quality of love you are radiating as completely as you can as you soul link. In addition, you can increase your radiance of love by emanating different qualities of light from your heart center to the other person's heart center. For instance, broadcast a smooth, reassuring, soft light through your heart center. Add a rose color. Make your heart light brilliant, or experiment with a pulsating light.

As you increase the love you are radiating, some people may not only respond to it—they may add to it. You can know this is happening through a feeling of spiraling up—feeling more joy, light, and love. This is one reward of soul linking: the fun of playing with others when they respond to and resonate with the soul love you are radiating. When this happens you have produced a shift in your and other people's ability to know their souls and to awaken their heart centers. Practice soul linking with many people today, increasing your radiance of love whenever it feels right to do so.

## Know *when to stop radiating love.*

At some point it will be time to stop soul linking. You will have radiated all the love the other person can use. This may occur almost immediately after you soul link, or it may not. Sometimes people will resonate and respond to your soul linking, and the energy between you will build. However, there will always be a moment when the connection between you is complete, and then it will be time to stop soul linking. You can know it is time to stop soul linking by paying attention to yourself. It may no longer feel joyful or easy to continue. You may simply stop, without knowing why. It may feel as if you are trying, pushing, or working hard to make a connection. When this happens, continuing to soul link can leave you feeling drained because your energy has nowhere to go. (The other person will feel fine, however.) Stop soul linking when it no longer feels easy. Know that you have radiated all the love that is appropriate at this time.

Do not look for specific outcomes or results to know if your soul linking is working. You cannot anticipate results, when they will come, or what form they will come in. Soul linking does not create a certain or guaranteed outcome, for you can never know how others will choose to respond to the love you are radiating. As you soul link you are working on the inner level, soul-to-soul. Working at this level can bring about positive and powerful changes in yourself and in your relationships, although you are not doing it for this reason.

You can radiate love to others without using the soul-linking images you have just learned. The steps given here teach you how to establish a heart and soul connection to others with a higher light guiding you. Once you have learned how to connect with others in this way, you can choose to use these images, create images of your own, or simply radiate love without using any images. Discover for yourself ways to make a high, loving connection with people.

The people with whom you soul link do not need to be aware that you are connecting with them. You are sending love to their souls with a higher light guiding you. When you connect with people in this way, you are changing yourself and your reality, not theirs. You are building a foundation of love that can later manifest as loving actions, words, and behaviors.

It is also fine if you want to teach others how to soul link with you. Then they can work to change their reality as you work to change yours.

Radiating love to others through soul linking is safe. You can never control others through your soul linking, nor can you be influenced or controlled if others soul link with you. When you radiate soul love, you are radiating the fine, beautiful energy of love. People can use this energy in any way they want, or ignore it completely. Radiating soul love is always a gift of energy that can strengthen, empower, and offer others an opportunity to awaken their heart centers and know more love if they choose.

If people radiate soul love to you, it is always your choice whether or not to use or respond to it. When people radiate soul love to you they are giving you the gift of love, which is always empowering. You may use it to feel lifted, expanded, wiser, or more energetic or loving. Thank others for the love they offer as they soul link with you, and radiate soul love to them in return.

# Soul Play

Soul link with people by making a line of light between your heart center and their heart center. Imagine the Solar Light above you, coming down through both of your head centers and forming a triangle of light between you. Practice soul linking with a number of people while you are doing various activities with them. Choose from the list below ways to experience soul linking.

1. Soul link and imagine that you are your soul. Observe any changes in how you feel, speak, or respond.

2. Soul link and sense other people's souls. Observe any differences in how you feel or think about them, actions you want to take, or what words you want to speak as you do.

3. Pay attention to the Solar Light above you as you soul link. Observe how the Solar Light enhances the harmony, beauty, balance, and clarity of your connection. Discover how your connection is becoming more beautiful and perfect at every moment.

4. Invite the Being of Love into your heart center in various situations. Note how you would act, think, and feel differently if you loved as the Being of Love in these situations.

5. Soul link and radiate love to various people, observing your own energy as you do. Continue for as long as you feel expanded and uplifted.

6. If people come into your mind today, soul link with them and radiate love rather than having any other thoughts about them.

# CHAPTER 9

# The Serenity of Love

*You experience your soul's magnetic, amplifying, transparent,*
*accepting, and unconditional qualities of love.*
*You know the serenity of soul love.*

All the soul-love qualities you will practice in this chapter to
awaken your primary heart center are aspects of serenity.
Serenity comes when you love as your soul does. You magnetize love rather than working hard to have it. You amplify
love instead of reacting to its absence. You stay neutral and
are transparent to the energies around you. You keep love flowing by accepting and allowing people to be as they are. When
you love as your soul, you love unconditionally, not needing
to receive anything in return for your love.

As you continue reading, you will have opportunities to
soul link and radiate qualities of soul love to someone special.
You can radiate the qualities of soul love to the same person
every time, or you can work with various people. It is powerful
to pick the same person to connect with as you radiate soul
love, for you are sowing the seeds of love that will later emerge
as positive changes in your relationship. If, after you have
chosen a particular person to soul link with, someone else
comes to mind, soul link with that person too. There is some
important soul reason you feel drawn to soul link with this
person while you are practicing a particular quality of soul

love. There will be something about this quality that will heal, evolve, or bring this relationship to its next level. Afterward, continue soul linking with the person you originally chose if it still feels right to do so.

You can radiate the qualities of soul love to groups as well as to individuals. Your heart centers are awakened through group awareness, group love, and group activity. After you learn how to make wheels of love in Chapter 21 with groups, such as your family, friends, and colleagues, practice the qualities of love in this and in the following chapters, and use them whenever it is appropriate in your group work.

Get quiet and ask your soul to show you the person it would like to soul link with to evolve your connection. This can be the person you previously soul linked with, or it may be a different person. Let someone come into your mind. If no one comes to mind, think of an important relationship that you would like to improve, and soul link with this person as you practice these qualities of soul love.

$K$*now that love is*
*the most powerful energy*
*in the universe.*

There are many energies in your universe—the energy of other people's wills, desires, and emotions as they try to get you to do what they want; the energy of your soul leading you along your path; the energy of the Solar Light that leads all life back home; and so on. You live in a world of energy. You experience and are affected by the energy around you all the time.

There is no energy more powerful than love. As you learn to love as your soul, you are bringing into your life the most potent force in the universe. Love creates miracles, heals all wounds, and purifies all lower energies. You cannot give love away, for the more you give, the more you will receive in return. When you choose love you bring about the highest good for yourself and others. Offering love is always the right choice. With love you can transform, purify, neutralize, lift, expand, connect, harmonize, balance, amplify, magnetize, accept, and add light and beauty to all the energy around you. You can transform or be transparent to people's emotions and thoughts, neutralize "negative" energy, and harmonize with all life in the universe. All energy in the universe responds positively to love.

*Be love. Bring love*
*to an ever-growing circle of life.*

To experience the serenity of soul love, start by breathing in, filling up with Solar Light. Calm your emotions. Breathe out any thoughts you do not want. You already know how to call your soul to you and blend with it without going to the soul plane. Additionally, you can blend with your soul and align your heart center's jewel with your soul's jewel simply by thinking of it. Call your soul to you now and feel its beautiful presence gently enveloping you. Its jewel descends through your head center until it surrounds your heart center's jewel. Feel the shift or "click" as the two jewels come into alignment. Picture beautiful light shining out of your heart center as these two jewels join together. Sense your soul as a radiant sphere of light all around you.

Soul love flows into your heart center as these two jewels come together. Imagine your heart center so radiant with love that love flows out from it, creating a field of love all around you. Love radiates outward from your heart center's jewel, going far beyond your body. This field of love that radiates from your heart center has many properties and qualities. The soul love that radiates from your heart center can be magnetic and transparent. It can amplify love, accept and allow, and flow out freely and unconditionally. From its serene center of love, your soul knows only peace and a certainty that all is well. Your soul knows there is nothing to fear, to defend against, or to get upset about. Your soul knows that love is the most powerful energy in the universe, and it knows how to love.

## *Magnetize love and all good things to yourself.*

Your soul is serene because it knows how to magnetize love. Your soul does not struggle or work hard for love. It experiences an abundance of love all the time. You can experience the magnetic quality of soul love and draw love and all good things to yourself. Sense the magnetic quality of this field of love that emanates from your heart center. Imagine magnetic rings of love spiraling out from your heart center, drawing love to you in all its forms, aspects, and expressions. As you radiate soul love, you are magnetic to the beauty and love within people and to all good things that the universe has to offer.

Many of the things people do for other people are for the purpose of receiving love in exchange. You may have been taught that love was something you had to earn through your good behavior and through fulfilling other people's needs. You may have trouble setting boundaries with others, thinking that to do so you might hurt their feelings or push away their love. If you think love comes to you only when you earn or deserve it, it is time to experience the magnetic quality of soul love.

Reflect on your relationship with the person you have selected to soul link with. Are you working hard to earn this person's love, doing things you do not truly want to do? Are you being pulled between doing what you think the other person wants you to do, so that this person will love you, and fulfilling your own goals, aspirations, and soul's directions? What do you think this person might do, or how might this person feel, if you stopped doing the things you are doing to earn love?

Sense your heart center, filled with your soul's magnetic love. It is not what you say or do; it is the love that is the essence of your being that draws people to you and keeps them with you. Fill your heart center with your soul's love. Soul link and radiate the magnetic quality of love to the person you have chosen. Feel how magnetic your love is to receiving love in return.

Translate your soul connection into a statement that defines for you the new way you are going to think about this relationship. You might say something such as, "I offer you soul love. It is the most important gift I can give you. I now magnetize the highest and best that our relationship has to offer." If it applies, you can also add, "I will no longer work or struggle to win your love. I will not try to win your love by anticipating your needs and filling them. I will honor your ability to fulfill your own needs." Take a moment to think about all the love you have received from this person. Appreciate how magnetic you already are to love. Recognize all the ways that you easily and naturally draw love to yourself.

Feel the difference between being magnetic to love, and working hard for love. When you magnetize love you stay in the center of your being and in touch with your soul. Love flows out from you and draws love to you. You do not send your awareness out to others to anticipate their needs and moods so you can then behave in certain ways to gain their love. When you are magnetic to love you stop doing things you do not want to do so others will love you. Instead, you do things that are loving to yourself. When you are magnetic to love you are not dependent upon one person as your source of love; you can receive love from anywhere and everywhere. You are serene because you know you can experience an abundance of love by radiating soul love that magnetizes love in all of its forms and expressions to you.

In this and in the chapters that follow, you will be given some suggestions of statements to say mentally to yourself or to the other person. They can assist you in translating the qualities of soul love you have just radiated into words. Revise these statements, update them, and improve upon them. Make them into affirmations to guide you in expressing your soul's love in your day-to-day relationships with people. As you mentally say these statements, notice any changes they create in how you feel about yourself and your relationships. When you say these things mentally, a different energy goes out from you. Whether or not others know what you have said, the shift this produces in you will change your relationships in some positive way.

## *A*mplify *love to increase it.*

Soul love is serene because it amplifies love. Your soul knows it can always find love in every person and in every situation. When you amplify love, you see the love that exists even when it seems to be buried, absent, or hidden. You can then act in more loving ways, even around people who are acting in unloving ways. You can assist others in awakening the love that lies dormant within them. Even the most difficult situation contains the seeds of love, just waiting to emerge.

Imagine going outside on a clear night to look at the stars. At first you may see nothing, then only the brightest stars. As you continue to look, more stars come into view until you see stars everywhere. This is similar to how your soul amplifies love. Take a moment and let your soul amplify and light up the love that lies within you. Just as you can see stars on a clear night, imagine you can see more of the love within you. Acknowledge all the love, compassion, and kindness you already express and embody. As you amplify the love within yourself, you have more love to offer others.

Blend with your soul and experience the field of love that emanates from your heart center as you align your heart center's jewel with your soul's jewel. Soul link with the person you have selected. Feel soul love flowing out from your heart center to the other person's heart center. Focus on the aspect of soul love that amplifies love. Imagine that you are making more visible all the love that is present in yourself, in the relationship, and in the other person. Acknowledge all that is good and beautiful in this person, both the qualities already demonstrated, and those that are emerging. Ignore anything you do not like about this person.

Make a statement that reflects your decision to amplify love, such as, "I will work at the soul level to enhance the love that exists between us. I now amplify love so that we may experience new qualities and expressions of love, find new ways to love, and bring love to new areas of our relationship." Acknowledge and appreciate yourself for all the times you have already focused on and brought to the surface that which is good and beautiful in this person and in your relationship.

You can soul link and focus on the amplifying quality of soul love if you have been fighting, if you are feeling rejected or taken for granted, or if you are having trouble recognizing the good in another person or situation. If there is a problem between you, think of this area as you soul link and radiate love that amplifies all the good and light that exists between you. You can keep working at this soul level until the love that is buried, hidden, or absent emerges. Working in this way increases your capacity to love and makes it easier to know what loving actions to take.

You can soul link and radiate the amplifying quality of soul love even if you already feel loving toward another, to take your relationship to a new level. You can ask the Being of Love to come into your heart center to assist you in amplifying love. Work on this inner level, and take action only when it feels right to do so. Amplifying and increasing the love between you and others does not mean that you need to interact with them more often or draw them closer to you. You can increase the love between you and choose to be with each person more or less, or to continue in the same way.

## *R*adiate transparent love.

Soul love is serene because it is transparent. Your soul offers love that does not add any of its own coloring to the energies about. Its love flows out transparently, without interfering with or being changed by the energies it touches. Your soul can be transparent to any energy that is not love; it chooses what energies to resonate with. You can experience the serenity of transparent love, a love that creates no resistance, does not add any of its own frequencies, and is not influenced by others' energy.

Picture yourself with the person you have selected. How do you love this person? Do you try to influence or change the other with the flavoring and coloring of your feelings and thoughts? Does the other person resist your love at times? Fill your heart center with your soul's love and sense a field of love emanating from your heart center. Focus on the aspect of soul love that is invisible and transparent. Imagine waves of transparent soul love flowing out from your heart center to the other person as you soul link. You are not interfering with or trying to change anything about the other person. Become the essence of love, a love that touches all life without interfering or adding any of its own coloring.

Think of a situation where you might be tempted to interfere with or to add your own energy as you interact with this person. Imagine radiating the transparent quality of soul love instead. You love without trying to influence, change, or affect the other person with your feelings and thoughts. You might create an affirmation for yourself such as, "I love you with a love that is transparent, not influencing you with my emotions, desires, or wants." Think of some of the times you have already demonstrated this quality, offering love without trying to influence or change this person.

How neutral can you be when you are around this person when he or she is upset or unhappy? How transparent are you to the strong opinions this person may have and any expectations of who you should be? Radiate the transparent quality of soul love when you are with this person and want to remain calm around strong emotions. Give yourself a statement that will be a guideline for you if you begin to react to this person's emotional state. You might say, "I am now transparent to those of your emotions I do not choose to respond to or resonate with. I choose what emotions I want to feel." Pause for a moment and radiate transparent love to this person. Appreciate all the times you *have* chosen how you wanted to feel, remaining centered, calm, and transparent to this person's emotions. Affirm that you can feel however you want to feel no matter what emotional state others are in.

### *F*eel the serenity of love when you accept and allow.

Soul love is serene because it is accepting. It accepts the universe as it is; it allows things to be the way they are. Your soul does not live in a world of polarity. It accepts the good and bad, the high and low. Your soul loves others regardless of how they live their lives, act, dress, speak, or behave. Your soul does not put up walls. Instead it melts barriers through its acceptance. Your soul accepts people as they are, no matter what their beliefs, opinions, or outlooks on life.

As soul love flows out through your heart center, experience the accepting quality of love. Feel your soul's love for and acceptance of every aspect of your being. Sense your soul's acceptance of all your habits, traits, and characteristics. If there is an inner voice that criticizes you, it is not the voice of your soul. It is a subpersonality who needs to be loved. No matter who you are, how you act, or what you say, your soul accepts and loves you just as you are.

Think of the person you have chosen. Imagine accepting and allowing this person to be just as he or she is. Reflect on some of the things about this person you already accept and love. Acknowledge how accepting you can be with your love. Radiate an accepting love as you soul link, until you can accept and love even more aspects of this person's behavior, words, feelings, and actions. Make a statement that affirms your accepting love such as, "I love and accept you as you are. I allow you to feel, act, and be any way you want to be." Feel the serenity of love as you radiate an accepting love.

If you feel resistance to accepting people, discover and evolve the subpersonality who does want to accept others. Start by loving and accepting this part of yourself. While you can love by accepting people and allowing them to be who they are, you do not have to condone or approve of what they are doing or how they are living their lives. You can still love and accept people even if you do not approve of their behavior. Accepting does not mean allowing someone to abuse or hurt you, nor does it mean staying in a relationship that is harmful to you. You can love and accept others at the soul level, yet choose not to be around them.

Notice how serene you feel when you radiate an accepting love. You stop struggling, resisting, or fighting against anyone or anything. You work for the things you believe in, rather than against anyone or anything. You love and accept yourself, and you know the serenity of soul love.

## *Love yourself and others unconditionally.*

Soul love is serene because it is unconditional. Your soul loves without needing to receive anything in return. Soul love is a quality of being, a shining light that lifts, soothes, and comforts all who come within its sphere of influence. Its love flows out generously and freely. It does not measure how much love to give by how deserving people are. Your soul offers love without needing appreciation, acknowledgment, praise, or reward for its love. Soul love does not come and go based on the actions or reactions of others. Your soul gives love to others without caring how others use this love or even if they use it. Feel the serenity that comes from giving love without needing to receive anything in return.

Experience the unconditional love of your soul by receiving its unconditional love for you. Your soul loves you without needing anything from you in return. It loves you when you are close to it and when you are not. Its love is like a river, a current that is always there for you to tap into.

Soul link and radiate unconditional love to the person you have selected. Have you been wanting something from this person, such as acknowledgment, or for this person to act in certain ways before you love him or her fully? As love flows through your heart center, create an affirmation that reflects your unconditional love, such as, "I offer my unconditional love to you. I love you without needing to receive anything in return." Think of a few times when you have offered love to this person without expecting anything in return. Acknowledge how generous and unconditional your love already is. See yourself expanding your ability to radiate unconditional love more frequently and in a wider range of circumstances.

When you radiate unconditional love you can feel serene, for you do not need other people to do anything in return for your love. You receive the riches of your soul when you give love generously and unconditionally, for all the love you give comes back to you multiplied.

# The Serenity of Love

## SOUL PLAY

Soul link and experience the serenity of love with various people and in diverse situations. Pick one or more of the soul-love qualities of serenity to practice as you blend with your soul and merge your heart center's jewel with your soul's jewel.

1. Be magnetic to love. Receive love from everyone and everywhere. Discover what you draw to yourself when you radiate the magnetic quality of soul love.

2. Let your soul amplify the love within you. As you radiate love, focus on the aspect of soul love that amplifies the love within other people, and the love that is possible between you.

3. Focus on the transparent quality of soul love. Radiate love without adding any of your own coloring. Be transparent to any energies you do not want to resonate with.

4. Experience the accepting quality of soul love. Accept all the energies you encounter without resistance or judgment. Allow people and circumstances to be as they are as you experience your soul's accepting love.

5. Express unconditional love; love without needing to receive anything in return. Notice how serene you can feel when you give your love freely.

6. Invite the Being of Love into your heart center and notice any differences in your ability to radiate the magnetic, amplifying, transparent, accepting, and unconditional qualities of soul love.

7. Love and evolve any subpersonalities who do not want to express soul love, feel it is too much work, or feel that others do not deserve this much love.

# CHAPTER 10

# The Oneness of Love

*Your soul stimulates your heart center. Light flows
from your heart center up to your head center.
Your consciousness is expanded.
You know the oneness of love.*

You have experienced the serenity of love as you soul linked,
practicing the magnetic, amplifying, transparent, accepting,
and unconditional qualities of love. You are ready to awaken
the heart of your head center, which I call your *head center*,
to experience the oneness of love. Love from your head center
is love that harmonizes energies that are different, frames its
actions in the context of how they affect all life, and connects
parts of the whole to one another. The oneness of love makes
the patterns of light between the self and others more beautiful
with every thought, word, and action. You may experience the
awakening of your head center in your daily life as increased
compassion and a growing desire to serve and to add light to
the world in some way.

Spiritual teachers call your head center the thousand-
petaled lotus because it has approximately one thousand petals
or energy vortexes coming out from it. Your head center looks
like an upside-down flower. The petals are pointed downward
toward your heart center, with the stem extending upward into
the higher dimensions. Your head center contains within it the

correspondence of all the centers below it. As you evolve, you raise the energy of all the centers below your head center into it, until all thousand petals are active and awakened. The very middle of your head center looks like your heart center with its twelve petals surrounding a magnificent jewel. The heart of your head center is stimulated into greater activity as your heart center awakens. As you radiate love, work for the good of the whole, and feel your oneness with all life, your soul pours more of its love through you, and your head center awakens.

*P*icture a stream of light
*flowing from your heart center*
*up to your head center.*

Join with your soul to stimulate your head center. Call your soul to you and watch as your heart center's jewel aligns itself with your soul's jewel. Feel the click or shift in energy as the two jewels come together. To stimulate your head center, your soul starts increasing the light it is sending into the jewel of your heart center. Light rises out of the jewel of your heart center and streams up to your head center like a fountain.

Watch as light flows back down to your heart center from your head center. As you breathe in, imagine you are drawing energy from your heart center up to your head center. As you breathe out, let energy flow back down to your heart center. If you like, sound an "om" as the energy lifts from your heart center to your head center.

Explore the way these two centers work together. Light from your heart center stimulates and awakens its correspondence in your head center. Light returning from your head center balances and expands your heart center, and makes all the energies of your heart center more beautiful. The light moving between your heart center and your head center is the first link between your heart centers.

*E*xpand *into the oneness.*
*Connect with the web of life*
*of which you are a part.*

While serenity is a basic quality of love as expressed from your heart center, expansion into the oneness is a basic quality of love you can experience as your head center awakens. As your head center is stimulated by your heart center, your consciousness expands. You become more aware of your connection to Oneness, to Spirit, to the All-That-Is. You grow more conscious of the life-force energy around you in all dimensions, up and down the evolutionary spiral.

Every aspect of love is expanded as your head center awakens, including your ability to feel the serenity of love. Your love grows wiser and more inclusive as you become conscious of the larger universe you are a part of. As this center awakens, you are drawn to do those things that make a contribution. With your expanding awareness and greater love, you join a higher flow, harmonize with the energies about you, and are in the right place at the right time. You become a force of love that empowers and serves the larger group you are a part of. Everything you do adds love, bringing back to you all the best the world has to offer.

Picture a stone being thrown into a pond. Ripples move outward, touching every part. Energy that affects one area moves out to other areas. Just as with the pond, you affect and can be affected by the energies around you, both those on the earth plane, and those in other dimensions. You are part of the oneness of all life.

Experience the expansion into the oneness that comes from linking your heart and head centers. Recall how you expanded your consciousness by focusing on the Solar Light when you journeyed to the soul plane. Start by feeling your connection to your family. Draw in Solar Light and expand your awareness, feeling your connection to all your loved ones, your friends, and then all the people you know. Continue to stimulate your head center and fill yourself with Solar Light. Enlarge your awareness to encompass people in your neighborhood, city, and state. Expand your awareness until you can include all the people in the world. Keep drawing in Solar Light and stimulating your head center with light from your heart center. Sense the animal kingdom and all the animals. Feel your connection to all the plants. Expand your awareness to include the mineral kindom.

Continue to increase the scope of your awareness by thinking of the soul plane and all the souls here. Look out into the sea of light and see the souls of humanity as points of light. Detect the soul of the earth as a magnificent, enormous, radiant light in the sea of light. Find the Beings of Light here—the Masters, angels, Being of Love, and Enlightened Ones. Observe their beautiful souls as they appear to you in the soul plane. You might notice that their souls' lights are so large and bright that they can be easily seen, like beacons of light.

You have now expanded your awareness to include more of a larger universe. This is the web of life of which you are a part. You are still an individual, yet your consciousness has expanded. Feel how vast your consciousness has become as you sense your connection to this larger group of life. Every time you connect your heart and head centers you expand into the oneness. Every time you sense your connection to the web of life of which you are a part, your head center awakens.

*Harmonize your soul's note
with the soul note
of a loved one.*

The oneness of love expands the harmony between all the parts of the whole. It brings divergent energies into greater flow, synchronicity, and harmony with one another. Think of all the souls in the soul plane, each one sounding a note, playing an individual melody. The note and tune of each soul is in harmony with the whole, creating a beautiful symphony of sound. Imagine you can sense your soul's note. It is playing a beautiful melody that is in harmony with the melodies of all other souls. As your head center grows radiant with love, your ability to live in harmony with everyone and all life increases.

Connect with your soul and let the soul-love quality of harmony flow through you. Listen with your inner ears to the beautiful note that is sounded as your heart center's jewel harmonizes with your soul's jewel. Let this smooth, balanced, and harmonious energy flow out from your heart center to all your subpersonalities. You are harmonizing them with the oneness and connecting them with the larger world that they, too, are a part of. Sound your soul's note and listen with your inner ears as your soul adds its note and melody to the symphony of sound that all souls are playing together. Feel your harmony with all life in the universe.

It is important to love and connect with the larger group, and also to love and honor each individual within the group. While you are in the soul plane, call to you the soul of the person you have picked to work with. Sense your two souls playing together in ways that expand the love and harmony between you. Harmonize your soul's note with the note of the other person's soul. Listen with your inner ears to the beautiful melody you create together as you blend your souls' notes.

Picture your relationship being in harmony with everyone you know and with all life in the universe. If you feel you cannot harmonize your soul energies, sense both of your souls as they harmonize with the souls of all life, and feel your harmony together at this level.

After you sense harmony between your two souls, let it filter down into your personality connection. Soul link and feel your differences melting away. You might say, "I appreciate you for the unique and special person you are. I will find the harmony that exists between our souls and bring that harmony into our personality connection." Soul link and bring harmony into areas of differences, friction, or disagreement. In addition, you might tell yourself, "I will find the gifts that our differences offer our relationship. I will put more attention on what we have in common and less on our differences." Take a moment to recognize all the ways you already work to create harmony between the two of you. Affirm your growing ability to bring harmony to this and to all of your relationships.

*Join with your soul*
*to make the energy*
*between you and others*
*more beautiful.*

The oneness of love expands and creates more beauty in all the energies, people, and life-force it touches. Imagine you are your soul journeying through the soul plane. Everywhere you go, you increase the beauty around you. You connect, bring together, and add to the unity of the group. You might picture all souls forming a mosaic or mandala of light—a beautiful, intricate pattern of ever-changing light. Wherever you go and whatever you do, you add beauty and light to the overall pattern.

Blend with your soul. As your soul stimulates your heart and head centers, imagine all the patterns of light within you becoming more beautiful, including the light in your cells, emotions, and mind.

You can work as your soul does to make all the patterns of light and the energy between you and others more beautiful. Soul link with the person you have selected. Picture the Solar Light above both of you. Watch as, at every moment, it is fulfilling its higher purpose by becoming a more beautiful and perfect light. Imagine that you, too, are becoming a more beautiful and perfect light. As you observe the Solar Light above both of you, sense the love between you and the other person becoming more beautiful and perfect. You do not need to say anything mentally. Simply soul link and work soul-to-soul to create more love, beauty, and light between you. You are fulfilling part of your higher purpose: to find light, to draw in light, and to radiate light to others.

You can play at the soul level to make the patterns of light between the two of you more beautiful if you want to improve your relationship and do not know what steps to take. Or, you can work at this level anytime to improve your relationship. This can set the stage for wonderful changes to come about. As you make the energy between you and another more beautiful at the soul level, it can create positive changes in your ability to bring about a more loving, nurturing, and harmonious connection to the other person. Areas you might not think to improve can become even better than you imagined. Areas of challenge might resolve themselves in ways you could never have planned, for your soul is creative and intelligent.

Finish by making the patterns of light more beautiful between you and the souls of all the life about you. Imagine that everywhere you go, you add beauty, order, and harmony. You enhance your connection to the oneness, and sense the web of life of which you are a part.

*Feel your soul's compassion
as you view people's lives
through their eyes.*

When you expand into the oneness and experience your connection to the web of life, your ability to feel compassion grows. As you experience and acknowledge your oneness with others, you can have compassion for their suffering, even if it is obvious that they have brought it on themselves through unwise actions. You are able to enter into the hearts of others and understand their lives through their eyes. You are no longer an outsider, judging, criticizing, or feeling separate from others. Through your compassion you have a strong desire to assist people in ways that expand their consciousness and connect them with their soul's wisdom. It is only when you can put yourself in other people's shoes, and see their lives through their eyes, that you can know how to assist them. Because they can feel your love, people are more likely to open their hearts to you, allowing you to make a contribution both to their lives and to their spiritual growth.

Imagine you are traveling into the oneness of the soul plane, finding the soul of the person you have chosen. Connect with this person's soul, feeling your oneness at this level. Imagine what this person's life is like as seen from his or her eyes. Feel your heart open to this person as you see life from his or her perspective, rather than from your own. What are this person's needs, challenges, goals, and feelings? Realize this person is doing the best he or she knows how. The actions this person takes are not directed at you. They are usually a response to this person's emotions, needs, or past experiences. You may not approve of this person's actions or life situations. However, you can still offer understanding, compassion, and assistance if it is appropriate.

Affirm your compassion when you are with others by saying to yourself something such as, "I am one with you; I am not separate from you. I offer you my understanding and compassion." Think of a time when you were kind, understanding, and compassionate. Acknowledge how kind, compassionate, and understanding you already are. As your sense of oneness with people grows, compassion will become your natural and normal response. You will soul link and connect with people's soul, asking what you can do to assist them at the soul level. You will not want to save people from the consequences of their actions, or take away the lessons they are learning. You will work as your soul does, radiating and offering soul love. As you continue to awaken your head center and expand your awareness, you will become aware of the wise, loving actions you can take that will assist people in expanding their consciousness and seeing new ways to act and be.

*B*ecome more aware
*of others' lives and concerns.*
*Practice self-forgetfulness.*

As you feel your connection to the web of life, you gain a broader perspective in which you, your life, and your concerns are not the center of the universe. As you enter into the oneness and see other people's lives through their eyes, you become more aware of the reality of others. Selfishness turns into selflessness. You let go of your sense of self-importance that separates you from others, and feel your oneness with them instead. As you do this you can experience greater harmony and peace in your interactions with others, for you no longer take their actions personally. You perceive the larger picture of their lives, and view their actions from understanding who they are and the lessons they are learning.

Play today with expressing the soul love quality of self-forgetfulness as you focus on others instead of on yourself. Have fun and notice the results. Rather than wondering what people can give *you*, wonder instead what you can give *them*.

Soul link with the person you have chosen when you are in direct contact. Let go of your concerns for yourself and your life, and be aware of the other person's reality. Discover any tendency to talk about yourself; do not speak of your concerns or your accomplishments. Ask about the other person instead. Only volunteer information about yourself if the information serves the other person in some way. Congratulate and acknowledge yourself for all the times you have already acted in this way around this person. Recognize all the times you have set aside your own concerns, feeling your oneness with others as you assisted and served them.

## *Contribute to the oneness by offering love to all life.*

You can know your head center is awakening by your growing desire to make a difference, to add light to the world, to make a contribution, and to serve in some way. The desire to make a contribution does not come because it is fashionable, because it will advance you spiritually, or from a desire for personal fame or recognition. It does not come from a sentimental feeling of wanting to make people's circumstances better just because you do not want to feel bad as you think about them. Assisting others does not arise out of pity. It comes as a result of soul contact.

Serving and empowering others is a joyous expression of soul love flowing out from you to the world. You want to serve because it feels natural, brings you joy, and gives you a way to express the love that is overflowing within you. Your service may or may not take an outer expression. Some people serve through working on the soul plane, transmitting love. Others work to bring about conditions that improve people's lives. If you do not know what to do to make a contribution, keep blending with your soul and awakening your heart centers. Work first on the inner level. Acknowledge all the ways you are already adding light and making a contribution to others and to the world. As your soul contact increases, you will draw to you even more opportunities to make a difference.

Your head center awakens every time you expand your love, harmonize with others, and add more beauty, order, and light to the energies about you. You know you are part of the web of life, and your love expands to reflect your awareness of the oneness and your part in it. Your compassion and ability to honor the reality of others grow. You are able to enter into the hearts of others and become a force of good and a source of love.

# Soul Play

Pick one way to awaken your head center from the list below. Experience the energy rising from your heart center to your head center as you experience various aspects of the oneness of love.

1. Expand into the oneness at least once today. Sense the web of life of which you are a part. Feel your connection to life up and down the evolutionary spiral.
2. Sound your soul's note and imagine that it is harmonizing with the notes being sounded by all other souls.
3. Harmonize your soul's note with the soul note of another person. Picture your relationship being in harmony with the greater universe of which you both are a part.
4. Bring the harmony you created at the soul level into your daily connection. Soul link and radiate harmony. Discover how this can soften areas of friction and can draw you closer to each other.
5. Soul link and focus on the Solar Light above the two of you as it becomes a more beautiful and perfect light. Imagine that the energy is becoming more beautiful between the two of you. Discover how doing this changes how you feel, act, and respond to the other person.
6. Experience life from the other person's perspective as you soul link. Express your soul's kindness, compassion, and understanding.
7. Focus on the other person's life rather than upon your own as you soul link. Have fun and notice how practicing self-forgetfulness alters how you feel about yourself.

# CHAPTER 11

# The Will to Love

*Your soul's will to love becomes your desire to love.*
*You express your soul's consistent, soft,*
*enduring, and patient love.*

You have awakened your heart and head centers as you joined with your soul and practiced the serenity and oneness of love. Experience next your soul's will to love, felt at the personality level as a desire to love. With your soul's will to love strengthening your desire to love, you can love in situations where you might have withdrawn your love in the past. You no longer *try* to feel loving; love becomes your natural response.

You can experience your soul's will to love by joining with your soul to stimulate the hidden point of light in your solar plexus center. This center has a bright point of light and a hidden, awakening point of light surrounded by ten petals. The hidden point lies within the bright light of your solar plexus center. Both affect your ability to express love, so I have included them as aspects of your heart centers.

The bright point of light is overstimulated in much of humanity, making the solar plexus center the most active of all centers for most people. The bright point contains the ego, desires, and individual will, out of which arise feelings of separateness, self-importance, and self-centeredness. For most of humanity, the hidden point is a dim, unawakened light. The majority of humanity does not yet act from their soul's will to love. Most of you reading this book already have much activity in this hidden point of light, for activity in this point draws you to your soul and to love.

*Observe as your soul sends light
to stimulate the hidden point.*

When you are ready to stimulate the hidden point in your solar plexus center, blend with your soul. Align your heart center's jewel with your soul's jewel. Watch as your soul sends energy to your heart center until light rises out of it, streaming up to your head center. Sense your head center growing radiant. You expand into the oneness of the universe, connecting with all life. Your soul next prepares to awaken the hidden point in your solar plexus center. Picture your solar plexus center with its ten petals surrounding a central jewel. The jewel is composed of two points—a bright point of light, and a dimmer, evolving point hidden within the bright point. Focus on the hidden, awakening point.

Join with your soul as it sends its will to love to activate the hidden point. Sound an "om" and watch your soul send its will to love from your head center to the hidden point of light in your solar plexus center. The energy of will sent from your head center might look like a spark, a line, or a waterfall of light. Imagine the hidden point growing brighter with your soul's will to love, increasing your desire to love. Practice this several times until you have some sense of, or are able to imagine, your soul sending light from your head center to the hidden point in your solar plexus center. Practice this movement of energy so that you can recreate it in different situations and at various times to increase your desire to act, speak, and think in loving ways. You do not need to force yourself to be loving. Instead, you can connect with your soul, stimulate the hidden point, and let your soul's will to love flow through you, increasing your desire to love.

As light descends from your head center to the hidden point, you have made the second link between your heart centers. (The first link between your heart centers is the line of light between your heart and head centers.)

*F*eel your soul's consistent
and unwavering love.

Your soul's will to love is steady, reliable, and always present. Your soul can be counted on to love, no matter what the circumstances. There is no mood, thought, or feeling that affects your soul's will to love. Take a moment to feel the constancy of your soul's love for you. It is always pouring its love into you. Imagine loving yourself as your soul loves you— with a consistent, steady love that does not come and go based upon your moods or thoughts.

Watch your inner dialogue for the rest of today or tomorrow. Catch thoughts or feelings that are judgmental or less than loving about yourself. Then, join with your soul as it sends its will to love from your head center to the hidden point, strengthening your ability to be consistently loving to yourself. Change any unloving thoughts into loving ones. The more consistently you can love yourself, the more often you can experience consistent love from others.

Think of the person you have picked to soul link with. How constant and steady is your love for this person? Has your willingness to offer love to this person been dependent upon your moods or whims? As your soul's will to love activates the hidden point in your solar plexus center, tap into the quality of soul love that is consistent, unwavering, and steady. Soul link and radiate a consistent, steady love. Make a statement to yourself of your intention to radiate love consistently and reliably. You might say, "I commit to loving you as consistently as I possibly can." Imagine loving this person as your soul does—with an unfailing and constant love.

Recognize how consistently you have loved this person, even during difficult times. The light of love may have grown brighter or dimmer, yet it has always been there. Think of all the times you have offered love, even when you have been tempted to withdraw your love. Acknowledge how consistent your love already is. Make a picture of loving this person with a love that is consistent and unwavering.

Think of a situation that in the past might have caused you to temporarily withdraw your love. Rehearse responding to this situation in a new way. Join with your soul as it sends the will to love to the hidden point of your solar plexus center. Picture yourself acting with love, even when the other person is acting in unloving ways. Imagine feeling calm and peaceful and being transparent to the other person's emotions. As you express your soul's will to love, your love does not vary based on the actions or reactions of this person. You love this person no matter how you feel or what is going on in your life.

It is fine if you do not want to feel loving toward someone. You may only be able to love someone's soul and not his or her personality. Because you also love yourself consistently, you may choose not to be around this person if his or her behavior is harmful to you. You can love others consistently while still honoring yourself, your soul, your path, and your own life. Do not force yourself to feel or do anything, including love someone! Continue to make soul contact and join with your soul to activate the hidden point. Express love only if and when it feels right to do so.

*Release your desires for others.*
*Experience the softness of soul love.*

Another quality of your soul's will to love is its softness. Its love flows out softly, offering and inviting rather than pushing and controlling. It loves in a respectful, gentle, non-intrusive way that honors the choices and paths of others. Experience the softness of your soul's love for you. Your soul is always gentle and kind. It never orders you around or criticizes you. It offers you new ways to be, yet lets you decide if you want to follow these new paths and choices. Watch how you use your will on yourself during the next few hours or days.

If you catch yourself forcing or pushing yourself to do something, stop! You do not need to force yourself to do things or to act in certain ways. Join with your soul to stimulate the hidden point to increase your will to love yourself. Treat yourself tenderly, with respect and love. Remember when you have treated yourself in this way, and how good you felt about doing so.

Your soul does not impose its will upon others. It has no desires for or expectations of people. Your soul gives others freedom to do whatever they feel drawn to do. Think of the person with whom you have been soul linking. Have you imposed your will upon this person to get this person to do what you wanted in some area? Is there anything you have desired for this person, even if it is something for his or her good? You can increase your ability to love as your soul does—gently, softly, and without imposing its will upon others in the form of expectations and desires. As you do this you free other people from trying to respond to your desires. You trust other people's soul and the universe to bring whatever is best for them.

Join with your soul as it sends its will to love to activate the hidden point. Let the softness of soul love flow through you and out to this person. Soul link and radiate a soft, gentle, nonintrusive love to this person. Let go of your desire to have this person do something to please you or to behave in certain ways. Observe what it is like to have no desires for the other, no pictures of what this person ought to do or be.

Recall a time when you lovingly released a desire you had for this person. Acknowledge yourself for all the times you have expressed love softly and gently, without imposing your will. Create a statement to assist you in releasing your desires for this person. You might say, "I now surrender my desires for you and my expectations of you. You are free to follow your own inner guidance and wisdom."

Take a moment to think of various people in your life. What do you desire for them? Identify one strong desire you have for each person. Then, imagine what it would be like to release this desire. Join with your soul as it sends its will to love into the hidden point of your solar plexus center. Soul link with each person and release this desire as you radiate a soft, gentle, nonintrusive love. As you do this, you are freeing yourself from the suffering you may experience when your desires are not met. People can release any buried resentments they might have been carrying toward you from times when you tried to impose your will or your desires upon them. When you love with the softness of soul love, you free other people to follow their soul's path and their own guidance about how to live their lives.

*Feel your soul's enduring love*
*for you and others.*

Your soul's will to love endures throughout time. Your soul is committed to love; its love is persistent and persevering. It sees every situation as an opportunity to offer love. It never gives up on loving people. Feel how your soul has always loved you, and how it will continue to love you. Think of the sun. It is always there, even if it is hidden by clouds or shining on the other side of the earth. Its presence is constant, steady, and enduring. Your soul's love is constant, steady, and eternal, like the sun. You may or may not feel its love, depending on the "clouds" of your emotions, yet its love is always present.

Practice the enduring, committed quality of your soul's will to love with the person you have chosen to work with. Join with your soul to stimulate the hidden point with your soul's will to love. Soul link with the person you have selected and radiate a lasting, enduring love. It does not matter what the outer form of your relationship is. You can love this person whether he or she is in your life or not, whether this person loves someone other than you, or even if this person does not love you in return. Create an affirmation, such as, "I will love you as a soul no matter what you do or how you act."

Loving others with a lasting, enduring love does not mean that you need to be physically around them or stay in a relationship forever. You do not have to constantly be aware of and continually put energy into them. It means that there is nothing they could do that would cause you to stop loving them as a soul. You may not like or approve of their behavior. However, you can separate the behavior from the person and love as your soul does, with a love that is lasting, persevering, and eternal.

*Experience your soul's patience*
*by being patient*
*with yourself and others.*

Your soul's will to love is always patient. It is in harmony with the timing of the universe. Imagine that you are the sun, shining out into the solar system. As the sun, you steadily pour out your warming light, watching planets develop over millions of years. You let all life grow at its own rate and develop in its own timing. As your soul sends light to activate the hidden point, feel your soul's patience like the sun, which is always patient. Your soul allows you to grow at whatever rate is comfortable and right for you. There is no rush or hurry.

Notice any impatience you have with yourself in the next few hours or days. If you find yourself impatient with yourself or your rate of growth, be patient. Remember that you do not have to change everything about yourself all at once. You can bring about lasting changes with patience, persistence, and perseverance. Most growth is gradual. Grow at a pace that is comfortable and feels right to you. Time has no meaning to your soul; the process of reaching enlightenment is as important as the goal. It is a great challenge to move from a lower vibration to a higher one. It takes constant attention to sustain the higher vibration of your soul and to establish new habits. Extend your soul's patience to yourself, and let things happen in their own timing. Have the intent to be more loving and take small actions every day to express soul love. Forgive yourself if you act in unloving ways. Loving yourself for who you are and honoring all your feelings is an important aspect of soul love.

Think of the person you have chosen. Have you been impatient for this person to change or grow? Have you been working or pushing to make things occur faster than they are? Join with your soul to stimulate the hidden point with the will to love. Become like the sun, patient and calm. As your soul's patience flows through you, give up any sense of impatience or rush. Soul link and radiate a patient love. You might mentally say something such as, "It is fine to grow and change in your own timing. I release you from needing to meet my schedule on anything." Love and appreciate yourself for all the ways you have already been patient and understanding with this person. Think of yourself as a patient, calm, and understanding person.

*E*xpress your soul's forgiveness
by forgiving yourself and others.

Your soul's will to love is forgiving. It forgives no matter what others have done. Forgiveness is easy for your soul, for it knows that some people are not yet able to be more loving, to you or to themselves. Your soul never takes offense, for it recognizes that people can only treat you as well as they can treat themselves. Make an effort to attribute good motives to the things people do. They are not usually trying to hurt you. People can act in unloving ways because they lack self-esteem or self-confidence. Their heart centers are not yet awakened. Do not expect those who have hurt you to recognize that they have done so and apologize. Forgive others as you would young children who do not know any better. One day they will have awakened heart centers.

Experience your soul's forgiveness by first forgiving yourself. With your soul sending its will to love into the hidden point, forgive yourself for something you did in the past that you still feel badly about. Let your soul's soft, consistent, and forgiving love flow into you. Receive your soul's love for you as you forgive yourself.

You can offer your soul's forgiveness to others. Think of the person you have chosen. Is there something you are mad at this person for, or something you feel this person has done that you are upset about? If you are ready to release these feelings and experience your soul's forgiveness, soul link with this person. Join with your soul and radiate forgiveness. You might make a statement such as, "I forgive you for anything I

perceive you may have done to me. I release any self-pity and
blame that has separated us. I forgive myself for those times I
have not been able to offer you love." Remember some of the
times you have loved and forgiven this person. Recall how
peaceful you felt afterward. Think of yourself as a forgiving
person who does not take offense at people's inability to
express love.

Forgiveness does not mean that you need to do anything
or take any action. It is an attitude of love that does not judge
and condemn. Forgiving others does not mean condoning and
approving of their behavior, nor does it mean that you feel
superior. Forgiving others releases the negative energy within
you, and frees you to love as your soul. Every time you choose
love, you are the winner. As you forgive others, your body
grows healthier, you feel better about yourself, and you have
more energy to put into yourself and your life.

If you want to forgive others and feel you cannot, do not
force yourself. Start by forgiving yourself for not wanting to
forgive. Then, join with your soul as it sends its will to love
into the hidden point. Feel your soul's love flow through you
until you are ready to forgive the other person, whenever that
might be. Forgiving others does not mean that you need to
contact them or take any outer action. Forgiveness is an inner
attitude that brings you peace. You are choosing to feel the
serenity that comes when you release any resentment, anger,
fear, or guilt you may be feeling.

*S*pread *goodwill wherever you go.*
*Be love in action.*

Express your soul's will to love by spreading goodwill
wherever you go. Soul link with people you meet. Feel your
connection to your soul and sense the souls of others. Be a

ray of sunshine bringing love to everyone you meet. Radiate soul love to strangers and casual acquaintances as well as to loved ones. Express love through your words and actions no matter how others act or treat you. Smile without needing others to smile back.

Feel your soul's love so you can love people no matter how they act. If people speak or think unkindly of you, practice thinking of them lovingly. Forgive them for their behavior and be generous with your love. Realize that people who act in unloving ways are often under great tension or strain, or are experiencing problems that they are not yet able to handle with peace. If people seem bad or harmful, do not focus on these qualities. Instead focus on what is light and good within them. You might even thank people who are hard to love for coming into your life, for they give you new ways to experience your soul's will to love and to awaken your heart centers. Speak positively, and uplift those around you with your words and deeds. Enjoy spreading love, for all that you give will come back to you multiplied. Acknowledge what a loving person you are, and how often you already offer love and goodwill to others.

# Soul Play

Join with your soul and connect your heart and head centers. Watch as your soul sends its will to love from your head center into the hidden point. Practice this until it is easy to do. Use whatever steps below are appropriate to express your soul's will to love.

1. Receive your soul's stable, steady, and consistent love for you. Watch your inner dialogue and change any negative thoughts about yourself into positive ones.

2. Notice whenever you use your will to force yourself to do something. Stop pushing yourself, and feel the softness of soul love that allows you freedom to do what you want and love to do.

3. Catch yourself if you are imposing your will upon others by desiring them to act in certain ways. Fill up with your soul's will to love and release these desires.

4. Renew your love with someone you may have forgotten by soul linking and feeling the love you have for this person's soul, a love that endures throughout time.

5. Feel the patience of your soul throughout the day. Be kind and patient with yourself and others. Detect and let go of any impatience or rush.

6. Forgive yourself today for something you feel you did wrong or could have done better. Sense your soul's consistent, unwavering love for you.

7. Forgive people today for anything they do that you feel does not honor who you are. Soul link and send love to their souls.

8. Spread love and goodwill everywhere you go. Search out situations and people to radiate love to.

# CHAPTER 12

# Surrendering to Love

*You lift solar plexus energy into your heart center*
*to be absorbed and transformed into love.*
*You surrender the lower to the higher.*

You are ready to make the third and final link between your heart centers as you raise the energy of the hidden point in your solar plexus center into your heart center. This is the link that you make with your personal will and imagination as you surrender those feelings and desires that stop you from expressing soul love. These arise from the bright point of light in your solar plexus center, for it is the seat of your emotions, desires, personality, ego, and identity. I will refer to the hidden point in your solar plexus center as your *solar plexus center* or as the *hidden point*. I will refer to the bright point as the *unevolved solar plexus center* or the *bright point*.

As you stimulate the hidden point with your soul's will to love, it gains in radiance. The hidden point begins to interact with the bright point, absorbing this energy into itself. You next lift the hidden point into your heart center. This strengthens your ability to surrender emotions and desires that would separate you from others and from your soul's love for you. As the hidden point awakens and your solar plexus center evolves, your emotions become calm and flowing. You have no fear, anger, depression, loneliness, self-pity, or blame. Each thought, perception, and belief becomes one that supports you in loving yourself and others. You do not want to control others, nor do you allow yourself to be controlled by others' emotions and desires. You take responsibility for making your life work. You surrender power struggles and conflicts, change criticism into appreciation, and transform the need to have your way into cooperation and support. You think, speak, and act in ways that contribute to the good of the whole. You experience true power, which is not power over people, but the power of group love, union, and cooperation.

Your solar plexus center is like a receiving station, picking up information about the energies that exist in the physical world around you. It registers thoughts and feelings coming from other people, mass thoughts, and even energies from the animal and plant kingdoms. Intuition in this center brings you insights and information about the material world rather than the spiritual world. Many of you are telepathic and feel other people's emotions in this center as if they are your own. You can change this by lifting solar plexus energies into your heart center. Then you will be able to stay calm and centered, sensing others' emotions with compassion and love, yet not experiencing them as if they are your own. As the hidden point awakens, you will use this center to sense the needs of humanity and the group you are serving, so you can put your time and energy where they will create the most good.

### *L*ift the hidden point into your heart center.

Begin now to lift solar plexus energies into your heart center to be transformed into soul love. Join with your soul, watching as your heart center's jewel aligns with your soul's jewel. Observe light flowing up to your head center, until your heart and head centers are connected with a line of light between them. Pay attention as your soul sends its will to love from your head center into the hidden point of your solar plexus center. As this point grows more active, follow as it interacts with and absorbs energy from the bright point. You are strengthening your will to love and your ability to surrender those things that stand in the way of love.

Lift the energy from the hidden point in your solar plexus center into your heart center. Picture your heart center as a radiant star or small sun above your solar plexus center. It is absorbing the energies rising up to it. You might want to sound an "om" as you lift energy from your solar plexus center up into your heart center. Light flows from the bright point into the hidden point and up into your heart center. Do this repeatedly until you can sense light rising from your solar plexus center into your heart center. You might observe this energy continuing to move up to your head center.

It does not matter if you can find or sense the hidden point. All that is important is imagining that you are lifting solar plexus energy into your heart center whenever you want to surrender unloving feelings, thoughts, and reactions. As you lift solar plexus energy into your heart center, you are making the third and final link between your heart centers.

## *E*xperience and love your feelings.

To surrender to love, start by recognizing when your emotions, moods, desires, and thoughts are arising from the bright point of your solar plexus center. These are emotions or thoughts that make you feel bad about yourself, deny your power, or cause you to feel separate from others. When you experience emotions such as fear, anger, guilt, shame, irritation, tension, worry, anxiety, depression, self-doubt, blame, judgment, self-pity, jealousy, or other negative emotions, you can know they are arising from the bright point of your solar plexus center. Continually feeling these negative emotions creates disturbance in your solar plexus center and devitalizes you. To transform these emotions, you need to be willing to feel them and to acknowledge that they exist. With this recognition, you can stimulate the hidden point with your soul's will to love so you can love your feelings rather than denying them, repressing them, or letting them control you. You can then lift solar plexus energy into your heart center to feel the serenity of love.

Pick one of the above negative emotions to transform, or any other emotion that you are feeling right now, or have felt recently. Join with your soul to stimulate the hidden point, increasing your desire to love yourself and your feelings. Lift solar plexus energy into your heart center to strengthen your ability to surrender those thoughts, feelings, and emotions that are not loving. You can love any feeling, much as you would love a small child that wants to be comforted and held rather than pushed away. You can know the serenity of love and experience your soul's accepting, unconditional love for you and your feelings.

It is all right if you are not always able to love your feelings, transform negative emotions, or feel loving and joyful all the time. Through the bright point of your solar plexus center, you can feel the constant outpouring of emotional energy coming from your own emotional body, the wants and desires of people around you, and the general emotional climate of your town, country, world, and all of humanity. Forgive and love yourself for those times when you are not able to stay calm, to be in touch with your soul, and to express soul love to others. Your soul accepts and loves you. Its love for you is constant, enduring, and patient. You will grow much faster if you love yourself as you are right now.

Certain feelings may be so strong that to transform them into love you will need to stimulate the hidden point with your soul's will to love and lift solar plexus energy into your heart center over and over. If you need additional assistance to change certain feelings, invite the Being of Love into your heart center. As you work with your soul, lift solar plexus energy into your heart center, and love your emotions, they will release their hold on you. You will be able to feel your feelings, love your feelings, and let them go.

*Lift solar plexus energy*
*into your heart center*
*to be transformed into love.*

Learn to recognize when people are operating from the bright, unevolved point of their solar plexus center. You no longer need to "pick up" or feel other people's unevolved solar plexus energy. You can join with your soul, experience its will to love, and lift solar plexus energy into your heart center to know the serenity of soul love. Doing this can change the nature of any interaction, transforming struggle, pain, insecurity, or tension into understanding and love on your part.

People who think in terms of winning and being right, rather than cooperating, are operating from the bright point of their solar plexus center. Additional examples are people who act self-centered, fearful, defensive, possessive, jealous, or controlling. Accusing, blaming, attacking, or threatening are also behaviors that arise from the bright point. Pay attention to how you feel when you are around people. If you feel less than, depreciated, or unloved, then the other person is relating to you from, or you are reacting from, the bright point of the solar plexus center. This is true even if the other person tells you he or she is being loving. Trust your feelings to tell you the truth. In addition, your body can tell you if you are around unevolved solar plexus energy. You may feel your muscles tense, notice a lump in your throat, or experience your stomach knotting up. You may discover that you are holding your breath, or restricting your breathing in some way. Or, you may sense general uneasiness or discomfort.

*Declare today that you are free*
*from others' desires for you.*

People who love through their unevolved solar plexus center may try to control you. They may use anger, disappointment, guilt, judgment, coldness, indifference, or criticism to get you to do what they want. Or, they may try to control you by withdrawing their love. You may find it challenging to follow your own path instead of doing what someone else wants you to do. You may be so compassionate and loving that you want to please others by fulfilling their wishes. Extend this wonderful compassion to yourself. Your well-being and your life are more important than making other people's personalities feel good.

As you awaken your heart centers and experience soul love, your love for others and for yourself increases. You will respond to others' actions with love, firmness, and clarity about how you want to be treated. Soul love offers love to others, yet it does not require you to stay in an environment that is hostile or unsupportive. You may physically remove or distance yourself from someone, yet you will do so with love.

You can lift solar plexus energy into your heart center to stop reacting to the desires, expectations, needs, and wants of other people. You can relinquish any resentments toward people you feel are intruding on your life or overstepping your boundaries. Think of the person you are soul linking with.

Connect with your soul, and ask to see where you are living out the other person's desires for you rather than your desires for yourself. Is the other person trying to limit or control you in some way? Is this person wanting you to act in certain ways to fulfill his or her personality desires? Recognize when you are reacting to unevolved solar plexus energies in this person. Lift the energy from your solar plexus center into your heart center. Soul link and radiate a transparent love. You might say to yourself, "I will follow my soul's desires for my life rather than live out your desires for me. As I do this, I create the potential for us to have a higher, more loving relationship." See yourself as the one who in charge of your life and your time. Acknowledge all the times you do follow your higher guidance and heart over what other people want you to do.

## *C*hoose love.
### *Surrender the desire to hurt.*

To surrender to love, you will need to pay attention to any of your own emotions, moods, or thoughts that might lead you to act in less than loving ways. You may need to surrender pride, a sense of self-importance, or the need to have your way, to feel superior to, or to have power over others. You will want to let go of those emotions that make you feel less than, inferior, or doubtful of your worth. You will want to train yourself to think about others in positive ways, even if you feel they have hurt you. You will want to bring about harmonious conditions through your speech, actions, and thoughts.

Discover any reactions to others that may contain even the slightest desire to hurt them. Watch your moods and feelings so you can still be loving to others even when you are experiencing negative emotions yourself. Stimulate the hidden point with your soul's will to love and lift solar plexus energy into your heart center. Surrender to love, and respond to those around you with kindness. Recall several times when you have done this, and how good you felt about yourself afterward.

When you feel others have hurt you, you may be tempted to hurt them in return. At first you may want others to feel the pain you feel when they have attacked, criticized, not valued, rejected, misunderstood, or disappointed you. When you feel hurt by others you may want to react with anger, withdraw your love, or retaliate in some way.

If it seems that someone is trying to hurt you, start by acknowledging and feeling your pain. Do not force yourself to feel and act in loving ways until you have transformed your pain. Lift the emotions you are feeling from your solar plexus center into your heart center so you can feel the serenity of love. Think of times you have responded with love even when hurting others felt justified based on their treatment of you. Acknowledge yourself every time you choose to respond with love even when others act in unloving ways. In addition, forgive yourself for those times when you could not or did not want to act lovingly.

Once you connect with your soul you can feel your soul's compassion. You will understand that some people do not know how to be kind or considerate. They are not really reacting to you; they are reacting to their own fears and to their past. People sometimes say or do hurtful things because they do not feel good about themselves. Your soul never takes offense; it understands that whatever others do that seems unloving is a reflection of who they are, not who you are.

Think of the person you have picked to soul link with. In the last few weeks, have you, in even the slightest way, had the desire to hurt the other person? Why did you feel this way? Were you in a bad mood or in the grip of strong emotions? Or were you picking up the other person's intense emotions? Did you think the other person was trying to insult or hurt you? Pay attention to the things that trigger unloving reactions in you.

Stop before you react in a hurtful way. Take time to love and honor your feelings. Do not try to talk yourself out of unloving feelings. Love your feelings, listen to them, feel them, and then lift them into your heart to be transformed into love. Take time away from the relationship, or create physical distance, until you can respond with love. It is better to be apart for a while, while you transform your feelings, than to be together and act in unloving ways. Wait to respond until you can do so in a way that honors both of you.

## *S*ay *to yourself, "I now choose peace and love."*

If you are trying to stay calm and loving, yet find yourself matching people's bad moods and acting in hurtful ways, do not feel weak, think you are a victim, or blame the other person for "giving" you bad energy. Forgive yourself for not yet being enlightened! Lift solar plexus energy into your heart center and feel the serenity of your soul's love. Think of times when you have stayed centered and balanced around other people's negative energy. Affirm that you have the power to choose how you want to feel.

If people around you are in the grip of strong emotions, soul link and sense your soul and their soul. Before you speak or act, you might say something to yourself such as, "I now choose peace and love." Keep lifting solar plexus energy into your heart center to surrender any urge to react in an unloving way. It takes great self-awareness and continual attention to be consistently loving and erase all desire to hurt. Not hurting others is one of the greatest challenges and a most important step to take to awaken your heart centers.

# Transform anger with soul love.

To surrender to love you will need to release anger. Anger can be one of the most challenging of all emotions to transform. It is the "fight" part of the fight/flight response. Fear is the "flight" part, and I have talked about transforming fear in many of my other books. Anger is the root of many separative emotions such as irritation, feeling superior or righteous, self-pity, and even depression, which is anger turned inward toward the self. Almost everyone feels some degree of anger many times a day. This may be self-anger, anger at society, anger at people who oppose what you believe in, or anger at friends and loved ones. Think of your feelings today. When did you choose to feel anger, if at all?

Anger is a force, an energy that can move you away from those things you are angry at. Sometimes anger can be beneficial, such as when it motivates you to leave a situation that is harmful to you. As you evolve, you will no longer need strong emotions to propel you into action. You will act from the calm, peaceful wisdom of your soul. Reacting out of anger takes away your true power. It is only when you speak or act from the serene, expansive, and loving perspective of your soul that you feel good about your actions and words. When you act with soul love you experience true power—the power of love, the most powerful energy in the universe.

Start recognizing when you feel angry. Sometimes you choose to feel angry when you are around the anger of others. When you feel anger that is out of proportion to the situation, you may be reacting to past pain that you have not yet resolved. You may feel anger because you are out of harmony with the universe or feel bad about yourself or your life. Or, you may feel angry because you think others have not been treating you the way you should be treated.

Stop and acknowledge your anger the moment it arises. Do not blame others for causing it. If you are feeling angry, join with your soul to stimulate the hidden point to increase your desire to love. Lift solar plexus energy into your heart center. Relax into the serenity of soul love. Let energy flow up into your head center and expand into the oneness of love. Experience your soul's wisdom, compassion, and understanding. You can feel the serenity of love even when you are around people who are angry, attacking, defensive, and functioning from their unevolved solar plexus center. Choose how you want to feel no matter what kind of emotions, thoughts, or energy you are around.

Do you have any hidden or not-so-hidden anger toward the person you have been soul linking with? Lift solar plexus energy into your heart center. Soul link and radiate your soul's accepting, transparent, and unconditional love. You might say, "I surrender any anger I have toward you. I take responsibility for making my own life work." Choose not to be a victim. Instead, affirm that you have the power to create any life you want. Recall a time when you transformed your anger and acted from a calm, clear, and loving state. Reflect on how good you felt about yourself. Transforming anger is a powerful step to take that will create positive changes in your relationships with yourself and others.

*R*elease irritation.
*Offer love instead.*

Irritation is a strong emotion that can be experienced by people whose solar plexus center is awakening and whose sensitivity to the energies about them is increasing. Many people experience irritation as their sensitivity to the disharmonious energies around them increases, before they have learned to join with their soul and lift solar plexus reactions into their heart center. As you may have experienced when you were around people who were irritable, irritation can be contagious. You offer others a great gift when you transform any irritation you are feeling into love. A joyful, cheerful attitude is a loving contribution to the well-being of others.

If you are feeling irritation, or are around people who are expressing irritation, blend with your soul and lift solar plexus energy into your heart center until you can feel the serenity of soul love. Forgive yourself for responding to the energies around you in a less-than-centered way. Radiate a transparent love as you soul link. Forgive other people for being irritable. Remain calm and play with radiating various soul love qualities, such as a magnetic, accepting, and amplifying love, around them.

## Honor yourself
### by setting boundaries.

Respect your time, your needs, and your spiritual path. If you find yourself unable to set boundaries, to tell where you end and others begin, if you feel other people's feelings as if they are your own, lift solar plexus energy into your heart center. Remember the times you did set boundaries and people still loved you.

You can stay in calm, serene states of love no matter what emotional states other people are in by radiating soul love. From this state of love you will do what is good for yourself and your soul, rather than what other people want you to do. Whether other people change or respond to your love is not important. Every time you offer love, you awaken your heart centers. Decide whether or not you want to continue to be around people who do not honor you. Believe that all your relationships can be loving, supporting, and enriching.

# SOUL PLAY

Practice lifting solar plexus energy into your heart center in one or more of the following circumstances to increase your ability to surrender to love:

1. Study and observe your feelings and moods today. Transform a negative emotion into love by lifting it into your heart center. Feel the serenity of love.

2. Detect unevolved solar plexus energy in people's interactions with one another and with you. Lift solar plexus energy into your heart center and feel the serenity of soul love. Radiate a transparent love.

3. Identify less obvious unevolved solar plexus energy by paying attention to your body. Note if you are tensing your body or restricting your breathing; use this as a signal to lift solar plexus energy into your heart center.

4. Discover what emotional energy in others you are most likely to react to. In meditation, practice shifting your reaction to this type of energy. Observe any changes in your ability to stay calm around this type of energy when you are physically around it.

5. Notice if you are reacting to someone else's desires for you rather than to your desires for yourself. Lift solar plexus energy into your heart center and follow your soul's desires.

6. Identify any urge to act, speak, or think in an unloving way when you are around someone. Offer love instead.

7. Discover what events, people, and situations trigger angry or irritable feelings. Lift solar plexus energy into your heart center and transform anger and irritation into love, compassion, and acceptance of what is.

# CHAPTER 13

# Soul Love

*Light circulates among your three heart centers,*
*lifting you into a state of soul love. You become aware*
*of the Universal Presence of Love.*

You have linked your heart, head, and solar plexus centers.
As you connect these centers and circulate energy among them,
and as you practice the qualities of soul love, you can experience an expanded state of love. You experience a state of love
out of which right actions, words, thoughts, and deeds can
flow naturally. People have described this state as cosmic
consciousness, unity consciousness, Christ consciousness, and
living in touch with Source. In this state, you feel your oneness
with the web of life of which you are a part. You can express
the higher ideals of your soul, serve others as your soul does,
and become group-conscious as your soul is. You can
receive and radiate the love of the Enlightened Ones. I will call
this state *soul love*.

To connect your heart centers with light and move more
fully into a state of soul love, call your soul to you and blend
with it. Sense your heart center's jewel merging with your soul's
jewel. Feel the serenity of love. Your soul sends your heart
center so much light that light rises up to your head center.
Sound an "om" if you would like. Expand into the oneness of
love, sensing the larger universe of which you are a part. As

energy and light flow between your heart and head centers, you have made the first link among your heart centers.

Sound an "om" as you watch your soul send its will to love to activate the hidden point, strengthening your desire to love. It is fine if you sense this energy passing through your heart center on its way from your head center down to the hidden point. With this connection between your head center and the hidden point in your solar plexus center, you have made the second link among your heart centers.

Observe as the hidden point absorbs energy from the bright point. Make the final link by raising the hidden point of your solar plexus center into your heart center, sounding an "om" as you do. Strengthen your ability to surrender those emotions, desires, and reactions to others that separate you from your soul's love.

## Circulate light
### among your heart centers.

Energy and light are now circulating among your heart centers. You can visualize light flowing among your heart centers in any way you want. A circular flow of energy and light is formed between your heart center, your head center, and your solar plexus center. (See illustration on page 124.) It does not matter how you visualize the centers; what is important is your sense of the energy as it moves upward and downward.

Feel your soul's presence as you breathe in and lift energy from your heart center to your head center. Your head center connects and balances all your centers. It makes the patterns of light among your centers and the way they work together more harmonious. Breathe out and watch as your soul sends its will to love from your head center to the hidden point of your solar plexus center. As you breathe in again, lift energy from your solar plexus center into your heart center. Each time energy passes through your heart center, your heart center's jewel becomes brighter and more beautiful. Continue to lift the energy all the way to your head center. With your next outbreath, send the energy down to the hidden point. You can connect your heart centers using this cycle of breath, or simply through picturing light and energy flowing among them. Energy and light flows upward from your heart to your head center, then gracefully descends in one beautiful, continual movement to your solar plexus center. Energy then rises up to your heart center, repeating the cycle of flow among your centers.

Bring Solar Light into the cycle of energy that links your heart centers. Imagine the Solar Light above you, coming down through your head center, descending into the hidden point of your solar plexus center, and then rising into your heart and head centers. Circulate Solar Light through your heart centers. Solar Light makes the link among your heart centers more beautiful as energy moves up to your head center, down to the hidden point, and back up to your heart center.

Invite the Being of Love into your heart center, and notice how this changes your experience of the state of soul love. The Being of Love models fully awakened heart centers for you, assisting you in experiencing the next step of your heart awakening. As the Being of Love joins you, observe your heart center becoming more radiant with love. Sense the movement of energy becoming more flowing and beautiful among your heart centers. Feel the serenity of love as you imagine how the Being of Love experiences serenity. Envision being connected to the oneness as the Being of Love is connected to the oneness. Let this connection with the Being of Love strengthen your will to love and your ability to surrender to love.

*Watch as your heart center
becomes a golden orb of light.*

Picture light moving among your heart centers as light of great beauty, circulating freely in a smooth, even flow. Say "om" aloud or to yourself several times as you distribute light among your heart centers. You are watching vibrating, sparkling light as it moves upward and downward. The light is becoming iridescent. Pulsating, electric light moves faster and faster among your centers, until there is a point when you can no longer follow the movement. All your heart centers are connected and energy and light are flowing among them. As this happens your primary heart center ignites with soul love. Its jewel becomes a golden orb of light, glowing, shimmering, and radiant. Your heart center looks like a radiant sun, with rays of light spiraling out from it, extending many feet beyond your body. Take a moment to sense the brilliance and beauty of your primary heart center as it has now become.

*Connect with the
Universal Presence of Love.*

As you awaken your heart centers you become more aware of the Universal Presence of Love, also called the Universal Ocean of Love. Once you sense it as you circulate energy between your heart centers, you will be able to recognize its presence simply by thinking of it. Look out through your window, or scan the area all around you. Imagine that with your inner eyes you can see a field of love, a living presence of love that moves in and through everything, including objects, people, plants, and animals. This field of love is an aspect of God, Goddess, Oneness, Source, and the All-That-

Is. It can be seen as a field of vibrating light. It can be felt as pure love. This field of love contains all the qualities of soul love, and qualities of love that are even higher. It accepts and allows; it amplifies and harmonizes. It is transparent, steady, consistent, and enduring. It makes all energies more beautiful. It expands, unifies, and connects. Take a moment to pause and sense this enormous presence of love that permeates everything. Sense its aliveness, its awareness, and its love.

You may have wondered, "Is the universe friendly? Is it for or against me?" Know that the universe is absolutely and unconditionally *for* you! The Universal Presence of Love is always present, working for you and your higher good. This is the divine substance of love that is the essence of the universe. Circulate light among your heart centers and merge with this presence of love. Let it embrace and enfold you. It is ceaselessly moving you toward the experiences and relationships that will open your heart. It is continually working for you.

As you connect with your soul, awaken your heart centers, and become aware of the Universal Presence of Love, you are waking up from the unconsciousness that made you forget who you are and have always been. It is impossible to be outside of this field of love, for it is a part of who you are. You are made of love. As you awaken your heart centers you are gaining consciousness, waking up, and knowing yourself as a loving being. You are not truly *becoming* love, for you already *are* love. You are releasing those energies that veil the love that is within you. You are reconnecting with those parts of yourself that know how to love. You are remembering your connection to the Beings of Light and the forces of love you have always been part of. As your heart centers become more beautiful with your soul's light, all that hides the love within you falls away, until you are a clear receiver and transmitter of your soul's love. You become the loving being that you already are.

# *Be creative*
## *in connecting your heart centers.*
## *Use your imagination.*

There are as many ways to experience the connection and flow of light and energy among your heart centers as there are people. It is fine if you cannot visualize, sense, or feel the movement of energy among your centers. Simply having the intent to connect your heart centers and imagining that you are doing so is all that is necessary. Your imagination is a creative force that acts upon your centers to create changes in them and how they work together. Breathing in and imagining light and energy flowing upward—and breathing out, imagining light and energy flowing downward—is a very powerful way to connect and awaken your heart centers.

If you can visualize light linking your centers, explore what colors the light contains. In addition, you may sense with your inner ears a sound, a hum, or a note. The colors and sounds will be different for each of you, for they will contain your soul's particular colors, vibrations, and notes. Some people sense a pulsation, a vibration, or a physical sensation of some kind as they connect their heart centers. You may or may not have any physical sensation. You may experience greater love, serenity, expansion, or any of the soul-love qualities you have learned. You may also experience a change in your perspective, as if you can observe yourself connecting your centers from both inside and outside of your body. Some people do not notice anything at the moment they connect their heart centers. They feel the effects afterward, even hours or days later.

Many people report feeling wiser, more detached, and more whole and complete as they circulate energy among their heart centers. They are less concerned about pleasing other people's personalities, and they have a stronger sense of what loving actions to take to honor people's souls. They have more courage to stop doing those things that others want them to do that they do not want to do themselves.

Whatever experience you have as you connect your heart centers is fine. Do not expect to feel enlightened and totally loving simply by linking your heart centers. Doing this will assist you to take the next steps on your path of heart awakening. It will assist you in connecting with the Universal Presence of Love so you can feel and act more loving toward yourself and others.

Your experience of soul love may change depending on the mood you are in, the people you are around, and the circumstances you find yourself in. You may have a stronger sense of movement and connection among your centers when you are in a state of meditation. You may simply note that you choose to say or do things more lovingly, yet have no sense of light moving among your heart centers. You may not have any experience that you can identify as coming from your awakening and connected heart centers. Keep circulating light among your heart centers and radiating love. Know that your heart centers are awakening as you do.

Now that you have learned how to connect your heart centers and circulate energy and light among them, practice doing this in meditation until you can more easily sense the light and movement connecting them. As you circulate energy and light among your heart centers, you can draw upon any one of the qualities of soul love you have learned, or experience all of the soul-love qualities simultaneously. Become familiar with the state of soul love that linking your heart centers can create for you. From this state of soul love you can act, speak, and take your love out to humanity in ways that are in harmony with all life. You can make profound contributions to individuals and to groups. When you act from this state of soul love, your actions can help alleviate the suffering of others. Your awakening heart centers offer others the opportunity to awaken their heart centers if they choose, simply through your presence and example.

*Circulate energy among your heart
centers as you prepare
to meet people.*

Explore the state of soul love that is possible as you link your heart centers and wake up to the presence of love that is within you. Make this link several times a day, in various situations and around different types of people. Practice linking your heart centers with light and energy when you are in various moods and circumstances, just as you practiced connecting with your soul around a variety of people, in varying places, and when you were in different moods. Notice the ease or challenge of connecting your heart centers when you are calm, versus when you are feeling strong emotions. Sense the Universal Presence of Love all around you. Tap into the power of its love to strengthen your ability to love.

Wake up in the morning and circulate energy among your heart centers for a few moments until you can sense your primary heart center as a radiant light that extends many feet beyond your physical body. Sense the love within you. Feel the Universal Presence of Love all around you. Then, think of the people you will meet during the day. Soul link with them, picturing the Solar Light above both of you. You are setting the space for a higher connection to come about. After doing this, note any new insights or feelings about your upcoming interaction with them. Invite the Being of Love into your heart center if you are anticipating being in a difficult situation that will challenge you to feel or act in loving ways. Repeat these steps when you are around these people, noticing how doing this can assist you in expressing soul love.

You can circulate energy among your heart centers and soul link with people in many different situations. Do this when you want to experience serenity, feel connected, expand your love, strengthen your will to love, and surrender unloving thoughts and feelings. Circulating light among your heart centers can make it easier to know what loving actions to take, and then to take them.

Distribute energy among your heart centers when you are in difficult situations, such as around children who are misbehaving, tense work situations, problems with family and friends, and any strong, unbalanced emotional energy coming from others. Link your heart centers when you are around loving, joyful energy as well. Experience your awakening heart centers in spiritual places to more easily sense your soul and the Beings of Light. After you have experienced the love that comes from circulating light among your heart centers, you can recreate this state either by remembering and using this process, or by moving directly into the state of soul love that doing this takes you to. Circulate energy among your heart centers anytime you want to deepen your experience of soul love.

## *S*erve people's souls rather than their personalities.

Most people will respond to your radiance of soul love in wonderful and marvelous ways. You will usually experience delightful interactions with people and receive many wonderful gifts of love in return. However, not all people will respond positively to soul love. Some may not respond at all. Others may react in unloving ways. Do not think you have done something wrong if this happens.

When you act with soul love, your actions will not always please people's personalities. Do not let yourself be controlled by the reactions of others. If you feel certain you are acting with soul love, let it be all right if people do not love or like you for your actions. You might think of a child who sometimes needs limits and to be told "no" for its own good. Your conduct may not make you popular; however you will know that you have behaved with love for the higher good of the child.

When you love as your soul, you are no longer interested in pleasing others so they will love you. You want to empower people, which may or may not mean doing things that please their personalities. Sometimes loving others as your soul means taking actions that they may not like or approve of, such as being firm or setting boundaries. If others love you only when you do what they want, it is not truly love they are offering, but unevolved solar plexus energy.

Be patient. As time passes, people will usually come to recognize the wisdom of your actions and appreciate you for your courage in offering them an empowering love. If they do not, you will still have the peace that comes from knowing that you have honored and served both of your souls.

## *Love yourself as you are right now.*

As you read about and practice soul love, you may have several reactions. You may feel inspired to express soul love more frequently. In addition, a part of you may feel overwhelmed or rebellious about expressing so much love. You may find a subpersonality who is fearful that being this loving might make you appear weak or vulnerable, or who is afraid that others would take advantage of you. There might be a subpersonality who feels that being this loving is too much work, or one who feels depressed when it sees how much more loving it could be. These reactions are normal. Love and evolve any subpersonality whose voice needs to be heard.

What is being presented is a vision of how you would love if you loved as your soul does. Look at how you respond to a new vision. Do you use it to inspire yourself, or to make yourself wrong for who you are? Do not make acting with love another obligation to add to your list of "shoulds." Love others because it brings you peace and joy, and because it feels good. Accept yourself for who you are right now, including your unloving feelings and thoughts.

Connect with your soul and feel soul love whenever you can. Each time you gain more skill at feeling loving in a wider range of circumstances. After awhile you will be able to feel loving without trying or forcing yourself. It can take years of work, even lifetimes, to experience soul love as consistently as your soul. Every single time you express soul love you awaken your heart centers.

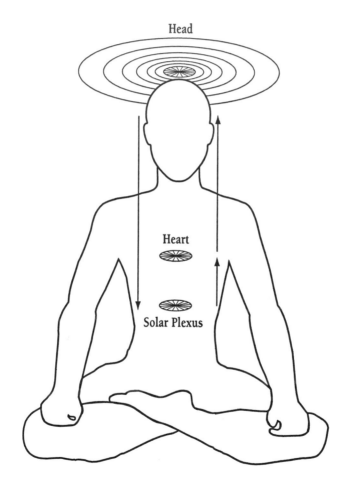

*Movement Between Heart Centers*

Soul Love

# SOUL PLAY

Awaken to soul love by linking your heart centers. Blend with
your soul. Breathe in, and lift energy from your heart center
to your head center. Breathe out, and send your soul's will to
love to the hidden point. Breathe in, and lift solar plexus
energy into your heart center, and then into your head center.
Complete this cycle a few times. Enhance your ability to
experience soul love in one or more of the following ways:

1. Circulate Solar Light among your heart centers to increase
   the beauty and perfection of the way they work together.
2. Imagine the Being of Love in front of you. Ask the Being of
   Love to transmit energy to you to further awaken your heart
   centers.
3. Experience energy moving faster and faster among your
   heart centers until you can picture the golden orb of your
   primary heart center radiant with light, extending many feet
   beyond your body.
4. Sense the Universal Presence of Love surrounding you with
   love. Affirm that the universe is friendly, and that it is always
   working for you and your higher good.
5. From a state of soul love, broadcast love to as many people
   as you can think of right now. Send love from the essence
   of your being as you soul link.
6. Move into a state of soul love and think of the people you
   will be with today. As you do, you are setting the space for
   a higher connection to come about.

# SECTION III

# Creating Soul Relationships

*You draw a soul mate
and other people into your life.
You discover the higher purpose
of your relationships.
You learn and follow
the universal laws of relationship.
You join with your soul to
dissolve obstacles to love.
You discover new ways
to love yourself and others.
You release or change
the forms of relationships
to match your new vibration of love.
You are in right relationship with everyone.*

# CHAPTER 14

# Attracting a Soul Mate

*Your heart center shines with the*
*magnetic presence of your soul.*
*You form soul-mate connections on the soul plane.*

As you awaken your heart centers and practice soul love, you
may want to draw new friends and loved ones into your life
who are responsive to your love, and who can match your new
level of love. You may want to have people in your life with
whom you are deeply connected, share a common path and
purpose, and can build a soul relationship. I will call these
people *soul mates*.

Most people have more than one soul mate. You may
already be in several soul-mate relationships with friends and
loved ones. A soul mate can come in the form of a life partner,
treasured friend, child, or lover. A soul mate can be someone
with whom you share a spiritual path, a joint work in the
world, or a commitment to be parents to certain souls. It can
be someone whose growth you are sponsoring, such as a child.

Your soul mate may be someone who has come to be with
you and learn similar lessons. Or, it can be someone who has
come to assist you in your spiritual growth by showing you
more about yourself and offering you ways to open your heart.
A soul mate can be someone who is connected to you from

other lifetimes and with whom you are continuing a well-developed past-life relationship. Or, this may be your first lifetime together on earth.

$D$*ecide whether to attract*
*an older, younger,*
*or same-age soul.*

I will define *soul age* as the amount of soul love, soul will and purpose, and soul light that people are able to express through their personalities. Soul age reflects the degree to which people are living as souls and the receptivity of their personalities to their souls. The age of a soul in the examples that follow is relative. You may be a very old soul, and a soul with you may be a very old soul, yet a younger soul than you are. Or, you may be with an older soul than you are, yet still be an old soul yourself. If you want to attract a soul mate for an intimate relationship, decide if you want to attract a younger, same-age, or older soul as your soul mate. Or, you can leave the choice to your soul.

Being in an intimate relationship with a younger soul offers you many opportunities to develop the qualities of teaching, serving, and empowering. Younger souls can provide you with a chance to pass on much of what you have learned and to recognize the growth you have gained. Being a teacher can be very rewarding when the younger soul is willing to grow and wants to learn from you. If the younger soul does not want to change or grow, you will most likely feel drained and frustrated rather than energized. If someone's soul age is a great deal younger than yours, you may expend much energy with few results.

In a relationship with a younger soul, you will have an opportunity to gain the soul qualities of patience and compassion. You will learn how to empower others without taking responsibility for their lives, saving them, or taking away their lessons. You will discover how to be in a relationship with someone whose vision is not as expanded or as farseeing as your own. You will be challenged to be loving, humble, forgiving, and kind. Younger souls sometimes feel threatened by older souls, and may try to reduce an older soul's confidence and personal power to feel better about themselves. If you decide to join with a younger soul, be certain that this person wants what you have to offer and is receptive to change and growth. When this is the case, you can find it very rewarding to be with a younger soul and watch this person evolve.

Most of you choose to be in relationships with souls who are of a similar soul age to yourself. With a same-age soul, you will often be growing at the same rate, and learning some of the same lessons. There is the potential for great joy as well as for intense conflicts in a same-age soul relationship. You will be challenged to gain the soul qualities of self-love. The degree to which you love yourself will determine your ability to love the other person, who will be reflecting back to you many of your own personality traits and qualities. A same-age soul relationship has the potential of being very intimate, for knowing the other can be like knowing yourself. You will need to be vulnerable and allow another person into your heart. You will want to love what you have considered unlovable in yourself as a way of loving the other person. You will gain by letting go of blame and self-pity, and by recognizing that you can only receive from the other person what you can give yourself. You will be challenged to calm your emotions and to know where you end and the other person begins.

Being in a relationship with an older soul brings different kinds of challenges. You might think that relationships with older souls would be the easiest, because of the compassion, understanding, and spiritual light they can offer you. With an older soul, you will be the student. You will be challenged to grow and to let go of any unevolved solar plexus reactions. If the soul you are with is too advanced, you may be called to grow at a pace that is too rapid for you. In this relationship you will have an opportunity to learn how to love yourself without judging, comparing yourself, or feeling unworthy or inferior. Older souls are often able to detach from personality reactions, offering you a more impersonal, wise love. This might not always be comfortable to you. The gifts an older soul gives may come in different forms than what you want, so you will need to focus on the essence of what you receive rather than on your expectations of certain actions, words, or behaviors. You will be with someone whose vision is more farseeing than yours, so you will need to learn to trust in yourself and develop your own inner vision. You will need to learn when to surrender to the wisdom and guidance of the other person, and when to be your own authority.

An older soul can offer much in a relationship, and can be a delight to be with. Older souls can teach you many things. They can make many valuable contributions to your life with their wisdom, insight, and perspectives. They can assist you in growing through the example of the way they live and think about their lives. As in any relationship, a relationship with an older soul has many rewards, as well as many challenges.

*Let go of thinking
your soul mate will fulfill
your every expectation.*

If you want to attract a life partner as your soul mate, there are several illusions you will need to relinquish. One is that your soul mate is someone you will be with for the rest of your life. You can have a soul-mate relationship that lasts a few weeks, months, or years. Time has nothing to do with the quality of your connection and its importance in your life. You may be in a soul-mate relationship with someone that lasts for the rest of your life. Or, you may have learned all you came together to learn and fulfilled the higher purposes of your relationship in just a few months or years. Do not measure the importance of a relationship based on the length of time you are together.

Another illusion is that there is only one soul mate who is your true life partner. You may have already had a soul-mate connection with a life partner, sharing a caring, loving bond that created much growth for you. Just because your outer connection has ended does not mean that this was not a soul-mate relationship. There are several soul mates who could be right for you if it is time for you to have a soul mate in your life. Who you attract at any given time will depend upon the lessons you need to learn and the higher path you are choosing. It will also depend on your soul mate's readiness to be with you.

In any soul-mate relationship, you will need to let go of the illusion that there is a perfect person waiting for you who will fulfill your every expectation and give your personality everything it desires once you are together. Do not expect your ideal soul mate to be someone who is always loving and easy to get along with, who agrees with everything you say or do, and who brings you a life of ease and comfort. You may experience your soul mate in this way at times, and at other times this person may challenge you to love as your soul does through his or her unevolved expressions of love. Soul mates always bring you growth and give you many chances to awaken your heart centers. Sometimes this process of growth is easy, and sometimes it is not. Soul-mate relationships offer you wonderful opportunities to work at the soul level.

## Determine if attracting a soul mate is your next step.

Before you attract a soul mate, you will want to join with your soul to find out if doing so is your next step. As you merge with your soul, imagine it lighting up the path for you so you can more easily sense your next steps. Circulate energy among your heart centers, breathing in, and lifting the energy from your heart to your head center, and breathing out, sending light to the hidden point. Breathe in again and draw solar plexus energy up into your heart center, then to your head center, continuing the cycle of light that links your heart centers. Fill up with your soul's love and wisdom. Ask your soul to assist you in knowing if attracting a soul mate is your next step. From this state of expansion, wisdom, and love, get a sense of the rightness of attracting a soul mate at this time.

If you do not get a clear sense that this is the right time to attract a soul mate, or if you have already been trying to attract one without success in doing so, work with your sub-personalities. Discover if any have fears or if they are in some way resisting having a soul mate. There may be a subpersonality who does not believe it is possible to have a nurturing, fulfilling soul-mate relationship. There may be one who feels it is protecting you from being hurt or losing your freedom. One of your subpersonalities may fear that a new relationship would take a lot of work and produce struggle in your life. Join with your higher self to evolve your subpersonalities. Ask them for their assistance and cooperation. If you are still not certain whether attracting a soul mate is right for you, stop trying to attract one and examine what is the next step for you to take. Ask your soul to assist you in recognizing where to best put your time and energy. Only attract a soul mate when you feel that this is the next step and the right step for you.

## Meet your soul mate
### on the soul plane.

When you are ready to meet a soul mate, focus on the Solar Light, letting it lift you to the soul plane. Call your soul to you and blend with it. Sense the sparkling lights of the many souls in the sea of light. Think of the relationship you want to call to you, such as a life partner, best friend, or child. Do you want to attract an older, younger, or same-age soul mate? Or, ask your soul to use its wisdom in drawing to you the soul mate who is the best one for you to meet and grow with at this time.

Your soul knows exactly what to do to call this soul mate. Join your soul in sending out a call to this person's soul. Then observe as one of the souls in the sea of light responds by moving toward you, coming closer and closer. Pause for a moment, close your eyes, and take in the beauty of this moment, the feeling of connection and recognition. Greet this soul warmly and feel it greeting you. You are with the soul of a soul mate, even if it seems as if you are just using your imagination.

The soul of this person is as delighted to be with you. Note how beautiful and magnificent this person's soul is. Discover what it is like to be with someone who amplifies your light, whose evolution complements your own, and who is here to learn and grow with you. Imagine that both of you are sounding your soul's note, blending your notes together into a beautiful symphony of sound.

Radiate love to this person's soul. Receive love as this person's soul radiates love to you. Sense the beautiful patterns of light you can form together. Play and enjoy being together as two souls. Mentally ask this person's soul if this person is ready to meet you face-to-face. Does this person need time to prepare for you, or is this person ready to meet you soon? An answer may not come in words. It may come as an inner feeling, sense, or knowing. Ask yourself and the other person's soul if there is anything you need to do to prepare to have this person come into your life. Invite your soul mate into your life if you feel you are ready to meet this person, and if your soul mate seems ready to meet you.

## *B*ecome magnetic to your soul mate.

When you are ready to call this person into your life, you can do so through your magnetic heart center. Let your soul fill your heart center's jewel with so much love that your heart center becomes like a magnet, radiating a powerful, magnetic love. Get a sense of how beautiful, magnetic, and radiant your heart center's jewel can be. Soul link with your soul mate. Streams of living love flow out of your heart center's jewel, magnetizing this person to you, calling him or her into your life. Add to this any image or feeling that you choose to call your soul mate to you.

Feel your and the other person's heart centers opening to each other. Whether or not you make a connection on the physical plane, you now have a connection on the soul plane. You can start developing your soul relationship, playing together as two souls. Harmonizing your relationship at the soul level will make you more magnetic to each other. It will usually draw the other person into your life more quickly and start your relationship on a higher note.

Meet here as often as you choose. Make this person a part of your life and build the love between you here that will be present when you meet in person. You can soul link with this person in quiet, reflective moments, or at any time you remember to do so. Circulate energy among your heart centers and transmit various qualities of soul love to this person. Review the soul-linking exercises in the previous chapters and repeat them, this time choosing your soul mate as the person you radiate love to. As you do this, you are building a soul relationship with this person.

## *B*elieve that a soul mate does exist and will appear.

Once you have magnetized your soul mate, you will want to discover any beliefs you have that may keep this person from coming into your life. Beliefs are conclusions you have made about the nature of reality. Beliefs can cancel the magnetic work of the heart, or they can reinforce your magnetism and assist you in drawing your soul mate to you.

Release any negative messages you may have been giving yourself such as, "There is no one available who is as evolved as I am, who is interested in the same things as I am," or, "It is hard to meet new people." If you have been working to attract a life partner and do not have one yet, release any beliefs that love is hard to find, that you are unlovable, or that there are no single men or women available. Do you have any beliefs that tell you a soul mate does not exist for you?

Work with these limiting beliefs to change them. Tell yourself that there are souls who are as evolved as you are, that it can be easy to meet a soul mate, and so on. Catch every negative thought about why you will not meet or attract a soul mate, and change it into a positive affirmation of why you can and will have a soul-mate relationship.

You can prepare for a loving soul-mate relationship and make yourself more magnetic to your soul mate by opening to receive love from all sources. Receive more love than you have ever allowed into your life. Practice receiving love from everywhere—from friends, pets, children, and everyone in your life. Let people love you. As you learn to receive love, you become more magnetic to your soul mate.

*Do things that make you feel alive.*
*Be magnetic to your soul mate.*

Once you have called your soul mate to you, do not put your life on hold until your soul mate comes. Are there things you have been waiting to initiate in your life, thinking that your soul mate needs to be with you before you can start them? Do those things now. Go hiking, camping, traveling and dancing; take courses; start a new hobby; and expand your consciousness. Do whatever makes you feel alive. Ask yourself what you think you will have with a soul mate that you cannot have without one. You can only receive from others what you can give to yourself. A soul mate will not make you whole. A soul mate will mirror any vacuum within you rather than fill it. If you want a friend, spouse, or child to give you more love, bring more love into your life now.

Once you have met your soul mate on the soul plane, and have invited him or her into your life, you may find time passing before you meet in person. At this moment, your path may not be union with another, but union with your soul. There may be more growth for you right now in not having a soul-mate relationship than in having one. Be patient. When you and the other person are ready, your soul and the other person's soul will arrange for the two of you to meet. Continue to evolve your soul connection, work with the other person's soul, and do those things you are drawn to do.

*Attract people with your*
*magnetic heart center.*

In addition to attracting a soul mate, you can work with your soul and your magnetic heart center to attract a variety of people into your life. These are probably not soul mates.

They are people such as doctors, repair people, employees, employers, contractors, teachers, sponsors, roommates, or others with whom you will have relationships that have defined or specific purposes.

Start by thinking of someone you want to attract. Imagine everything you can about this person: what skills, intelligence, creativity, spiritual development, loving manner, honesty and integrity, proximity, availability, period of time you want this person in your life, and so on. Think of the outcome you want, and picture this person being able to work together with you to achieve it.

When you have a sense of who this person might be and the qualities you would like this person to have, connect with your soul. Align your heart center's jewel with your soul's jewel. Ask your soul to fill your heart center with its magnetic love until it becomes like a magnet. Soul link with this person, sensing the connection between your heart centers. Feel the Solar Light above you, drawing you together in higher purpose. Ask and invite this person to come into your life.

If you have a list of potential names of the people you are trying to decide on bringing into your life for a specific purpose, soul link with each person. Use your imagination to sense which people feel the best as you soul link with them. There are no right or wrong choices. Each person will offer you different kinds of lessons and various paths of growth. When you find one or two people who appeal to you at this level, become magnetic with your soul's love, soul link, and invite these people into your life.

# Soul Play

Pick from the list below some area you would like to work on to attract a soul mate:

1. Blend with your soul, and ask it to assist you in knowing if attracting a soul mate is your next step. If it is not, explore what *is* your next step.

2. If attracting a soul mate is not your next step, discover how you are growing in ways that are preparing you to have a soul-mate relationship.

3. Uncover and evolve a subpersonality who is not sure it wants a soul mate, or whose fears are holding you back from attracting one.

4. Discover and examine one belief about relationships that you may need to change to attract a soul mate. Create a positive statement about relationships and repeat it often.

5. Join with your soul mate on the soul plane. Play together as two souls to deepen your connection. Welcome your soul mate into your life.

6. Evolve your relationship with your soul mate on the soul plane. Radiate various qualities of soul love as you soul link. Receive love from the other person's soul. Send a telepathic message. Receive an answer. Be as inventive as you can as you play as souls together.

7. Soul link with your soul mate, and feel your magnetic heart center. Invite your soul mate into your life.

8. Think of something you have been postponing until you have a soul mate. Resolve to do it now, so you can increase your aliveness and become even more magnetic to your soul mate.

# Chapter 15

# Discovering the Higher Purpose of a Relationship

*You take your relationship into the oneness
and frame it in the picture frame of the universe.
You bring the Solar Light of higher purpose
into your relationships.*

Relationships are a very important area to evolve as a part of your path to enlightenment and to living as a soul. They offer you a place to practice opening your heart and expressing soul love. They give you feedback and mirror for you the qualities you are developing in yourself. Relationships provide you with opportunities to love others as your soul does. They can show you all the places where you are still working to gain the peace, love, and joy of your soul. Every choice you make to offer love rather than to close your heart brings you closer to your soul. Relationships can assist you in developing qualities that make you a leader, teacher, or healer. Your connections to others offer you the opportunity to experience and develop your soul's infinite compassion, forgiveness, and wisdom.

Building soul relationships with your friends and loved ones can bring you many rewards. Joy exists when people's hearts are in harmony and when they are aligned in higher purpose. The deep desire to feel close to people is one of the most basic of human needs, whether it is between parent and child, two lovers, or good friends. You can feel pleasure, security, and a great delight in living when your relationships come together at the level that is possible when you love as your soul does. As you awaken your heart centers you can surrender any fear you may have of getting close to people, of being hurt, or of being affected by other people's negativity. You can choose to experience people as good and the universe as friendly. You can choose to live with joy and release the struggle in your relationships.

The most important work you can do to build soul relationships is to work soul-to-soul. You have already been doing this when you soul linked, focused on your soul and the other person's soul, and radiated qualities of soul love. All outer expressions of love are born from the essence of love that exists between you and others at the soul level.

## Realize that all your relationships have a higher purpose.

To build soul relationships, you will want to know more about your higher purpose in being together. These are the soul reasons you are in a relationship with people. One of your soul's purposes in being together may be to grow spiritually or to create things together that add more light to the world. You may be together to expand your ability to love and to experience all the growth you have to offer each other. Your purpose may be to guide a child's growth, and to grow yourself as you do.

Pick someone who is special in your life to work on with the processes that follow. Perhaps you will want to continue working with the person you have already soul linked with.

Get quiet for a moment, and let someone come into your mind with whom you want to connect in the chapters that follow to create a soul relationship. This can be the same person for all the processes, or various people who come into your mind. After you complete this process with one person, use it to discover more about the higher purpose of each of your important relationships.

*Discover the higher purpose of an important relationship.*

When you have someone in mind, call your soul to you. Merge with your soul and align your heart center's jewel with your soul's jewel. Connect your heart centers and circulate energy and light among them. Breathe in, and lift energy from your heart center to your head center, feeling the serenity and oneness of love. As you breathe out, join with your soul to send its will to love into the hidden point. Breathe in, lifting solar plexus energy up to your heart center to surrender to love. Picture energy circulating among your heart centers until you feel yourself moving into a state of soul love and can sense your heart center as a radiant orb of light.

Soul link with the person you selected, sensing the other person's soul. Envision your relationship being in harmony with the oneness of all life. Connect with the Universal Presence of Love, feeling the love that is all about you. Think of all the love your relationship will add to those around you. Picture the Solar Light pouring its light of higher purpose into both of you.

To discover more about the higher purposes of your relationship, ask yourself and your soul such questions as: "What have we come together to learn, to create, and to bring to the world? What is this relationship teaching us? What soul qualities are we developing? How is this relationship assisting us in growing stronger, more whole and complete within? What are our souls' purposes for our being together?" Ask your soul to show you what contribution you are making to this person's soul. What are the most important gifts you are giving this person? What are you teaching this person? What are you learning from this person? Take time to reflect on the time, love, and energy you have already given to this relationship. As you look through your soul's eyes you will find that these are your most important contributions—the gifts of your heart.

While you soul link, focus on the Solar Light and let its light of higher purpose highlight for you the soul reasons you are in this relationship. Work with the Solar Light to reveal more about what the two of you have come together to give birth to or to learn from each other. Commit to discovering and fulfilling your higher purposes for being in this relationship. Soul link to bring higher purpose to your relationship on a daily basis.

As you ask your soul to show you more about the higher purpose of your relationship, you may receive a feeling, symbol, or new idea. Your soul has many ways to talk to you. Your soul may show you more about the higher purposes of this relationship through insights, dreams, or things you read. You may receive information at some future time when you least expect it, such as when you are in the shower or relaxing. Or, you may simply act in ways at certain moments that reflect your higher purpose in being together without even knowing what it is.

Whenever you are with people, even a casual acquaintance, soul link and imagine the Solar Light above both of you, assisting you in fulfilling the higher purpose of your interaction at that moment. Your higher purpose in being with this person may simply be to radiate love.

# Create a soul vision
## for all your relationships.

One way to manifest the higher purposes of any relationship is by stating them to yourself and in writing. When you write out the higher purposes of a relationship, you are creating a vision to remember and work toward. This vision can assist you in remembering your soul purposes in being together even when you are absorbed in the details of daily living. A vision statement can assist you in fulfilling the potential of your relationship, learning what you came to learn, and enhancing the light and love that both of you are capable of expressing. The more you focus on the true purposes of your relationships, the more rewarding and fulfilling all your relationships will be.

To develop a vision of your higher purpose, think of the person you have selected. Soul link with the Solar Light of higher purpose flowing into both of you. Let one idea of your higher purpose in being together come into your mind. If this comes as a sense, thought, or feeling of energy, that is fine; let that be your vision. If you can, put your ideas about your higher purpose in being together into words. Challenge yourself to expand your vision of what is possible. Include the essence of what you want and the qualities you want to develop. There are many wonderful visions you can hold of any relationship. Trust that whatever ideas come into your mind are the right ones for you to focus on. If nothing comes to mind, begin by working with some of the possible visions that follow. Devise your own, be inventive, and have fun! Possible relationship visions and affirmations:

✧ This relationship contributes to our spiritual growth and to manifesting our higher purposes.

✧ This relationship supports our soul contact, soul love, and soul growth.

✧ I see what is good, strong, and beautiful in you, in myself, and in our relationship.

✧ I work as a team with you, manifesting our common goals and shared visions.

✧ I commit to our joint work together.

✧ I deepen our relationship by first contacting my soul and soul linking, letting the outer forms follow from the inner essence of love.

✧ I learn what I need to learn from this relationship through joy rather than through struggle.

✧ I commit to maintaining a soul connection no matter what form our relationship may take.

✧ Our relationship strengthens, inspires, and empowers both of us to become all that we are capable of being.

✧ I nourish and guide your development in ways that honor your essence and bring you closer to your soul.

After you have formulated a vision that reflects the soul purposes of your relationship, put your vision statement someplace where you can be reminded of it frequently. Every time you look at your vision statement, you add energy to it so it can manifest in your life. If possible, talk about your vision with the other person and refine it together.

If the other person is not interested in or is unable to work with you to discover and create a vision, feel free to discover and energize those visions that fit your own purposes for being in the relationship. When you soul link with this person, radiate a transparent and accepting love, so there is no pressure for the other person to change to meet your vision.

Use this vision as something to strive for; do not make yourself wrong for not yet having it. It takes time for visions to become reality. As you create a vision, you are creating your future relationship. You are expanding the potential love and joy your relationship can bring you.

### *B*elieve in your ability
### to create soul relationships.

After you have explored and created a vision of the higher purposes of a relationship, you will want to uncover beliefs that may be holding you back from making this vision a reality. These may be beliefs that lock you into old ways of relating or keep you from experiencing the full potential of your relationship. Explore your beliefs about relationships if you find it challenging to manifest your higher purpose and vision, if you find unwanted relationship patterns repeating no matter how much soul linking you do, or if you sense yourself reacting in old ways even when you want to change.

Get quiet and connect with your soul. Ask it to show you any beliefs you might need to alter to fulfill the higher purpose of your relationship. The Solar Light is shining above you, assisting you in bringing to light any beliefs that need to be examined. You can look at what you have experienced in past and present relationships, and let this show you more about what you believe to be true about relationships. Have certain patterns been repeating themselves? If so, ask, "What would I need to believe about people or relationships for these experiences to occur in my life?" These are beliefs you have about relationships that you can transform.

For example, you may believe that relationships start off the best they will ever be and deteriorate thereafter. You may believe that you will repeat your parents' mistakes with your own children. Perhaps you believe that good friendships do not really exist or that relationships take a lot of work. You may believe that you are not lovable, that it is not possible to have your needs met, or that other people are not interested in building a soul relationship with you. As you change your beliefs, you will transform what you experience.

If you discover a limiting belief, alter it by telling yourself the opposite, turning it into a positive statement. For instance, if you discover a belief such as, "I will never have my needs met in a relationship," change it to "I can create relationships that are fulfilling." Find a belief that may be holding you back from building a soul relationship with someone. Feel your soul's presence as you blend with your soul and circulate energy among your heart centers. Think of one of the higher purposes of your relationship. You might complete the sentence, "I believe it might be difficult to create my higher purpose in this relationship with [name] because _____." Soul link and imagine the two of you being linked in higher purpose. Say something positive to yourself such as, "I now believe we can fulfill our higher purpose together because _____." When you soul link and connect soul-to-soul, focusing on discovering and living the higher purpose of your relationship, you can create rewarding, fulfilling soul relationships with everyone in your life.

## Discovering the Higher Purpose of a Relationship

# SOUL PLAY

Create a soul vision for each important relationship. Start by blending with your soul. Circulate energy among your heart centers. Soul link, sensing your soul and the other person's soul. Feel the Solar Light amplifying the higher purpose of your relationship. View your relationship from the perspective of the greater universe of which you both are a part.

To discover more about the higher purposes of your relationship, ask yourself and your soul such questions as: "What have we come together to learn, to create, and to bring to the world? What is this relationship teaching us? What soul qualities are we developing? How is this relationship assisting us in growing stronger, more whole and complete within? What are our souls' purposes for our being together?" Create a soul vision of one of the higher purposes of your being in a relationship with:

- Your most important loved one.
- A special child, such as your child, grandchild, niece, or nephew.
- A parent, grandparent, aunt, or uncle.
- A brother or sister.
- Your best friend, or another friend.
- A colleague, employee, or employer.
- Anyone else who is important in your life.

Write out a vision of at least one of the higher purposes of each relationship you chose. Affirm your belief in your ability to create this higher purpose.

# CHAPTER 16

# Creating the Relationship You Want

*You create the relationships you want by following
the universal laws of relationship.
The outer mirrors the inner.*

You have been creating a soul relationship with someone as you focused on the higher purpose of your relationship, developed a vision, and examined your beliefs. You can take the next steps of creating a soul relationship by learning and following the universal laws of relationship. When you understand and follow these principles, you can create the relationship you want.

You may be trying to find or create perfect love in your life. Pure, clear, true love exists at the soul level, between souls. Even the most understanding person will not always be able to love you the way your personality wants to be loved. Some may come close, yet there will always be places where you do not feel completely loved, understood, or appreciated. With this knowledge, you can be more understanding and forgiving of others, knowing that there is no way they could ever completely satisfy you.

You can stop looking for the perfect person to love, or stop trying to change the people you are with to make them please you more. Instead, you can look at how what you are experiencing in a relationship mirrors something that is occurring within yourself.

*K*now the essence of what you want.
*When you have the essence,*
*many forms will work.*

A universal law of relationships is that to create the relationship you want, you need to focus on creating the essence of what you want, rather than on a specific form. What is essence? It is a feeling, a soul quality; it is the soul love you want. When the essence is missing, no form will work. When it is present, many forms will work. For instance, the essence of what you want may be a caring, loving connection. You think you will experience this if someone takes you out and spends time with you—a specific form. However, if this person takes you out and does not make a loving connection, the form of "going out" will not bring you what you want. Yet, if this person makes a wonderful, loving connection with you, many forms will work, even staying at home.

People often have specific pictures of what actions others must take to show their love. You may want someone to show love for you by behaving in specific ways, such as by listening to you attentively, by giving you affection, or by appreciating you. You may want your children to help with the chores, pay attention, follow your suggestions, or act in certain ways to please you. You may want your friends to see you at certain intervals, respond to your phone calls, or be available to spend time with you. You may want your spouse or partner to give you more support with the finances, surprise you with gifts, take you to special places, or listen attentively to you.

No outer forms will bring you lasting joy. The personality is never happy for long. When some of its desires are filled, it comes up with a list of new ones! When you open to receive the essence of what you want rather than needing love to come in a specific form, love can come to you from anyone and everyone, bringing you true joy and lasting happiness.

Ask yourself, "What feelings, what qualities of love do I want in this relationship?" These might be feelings of serenity, softness, connection, or harmony. Join with your soul to bring these feelings and qualities of love into yourself as you distribute energy among your heart centers. Breathe in, lifting energy from your heart center to your head center to feel the serenity and oneness of love. Breathe out, sending light from your head center to the hidden point to strengthen your will to love. Breathe in again and draw solar plexus energy into your heart center to surrender to love. Feel the Universal Presence of Love all around you, enhancing your ability to express love.

Think of the person you have chosen. Soul link and radiate the qualities of soul love you want to experience in your relationship. Ask your soul to assist you in receiving insights about new ways you could be together that would support you in experiencing these qualities of love. As you picture these qualities manifesting in your connections with this person, they will. When you create the soul qualities of love in your relationship, the forms and structures that match will naturally evolve.

Look beyond the specific ways you want to receive love from this person and notice whether this person is offering you love in ways you have not been aware of. People do not usually deny you what you want because they are trying to hurt you or withhold love from you. Often they are giving you love in the way they were given love, or in the way they want to receive it. Even when you request it, they still may not be able to express love in the way you want, for that behavior is unfamiliar to them. It may seem unnatural, or they may have trouble believing it means so much to you. You can grow closer to people by letting go of needing to receive love in a particular way, and finding the essence of love between you.

Recognize all the ways people are giving you the essence of love, perhaps in ways that you might not have noticed or acknowledged. Thank people for every gift of love they offer you. Do not rely on gestures or outer appearances as an indication of the love that people have for you. Rely instead on the feeling of love that exists between you.

## *Believe in your ability to create the relationship you want.*

An important principle in creating the relationship you want is that you need to believe that you *can* create what you want. You will need to release any feelings that you are a victim, including feelings of self-pity, blame, or thoughts that you cannot have what you want because someone is stopping you. Is there anyone you have been blaming for your life not working? Do you feel someone is holding you back, taking away your freedom, or causing problems in your life? Claim your true power to create the life you want! Remember a time when you let go of being a victim or blaming someone and took action to create what you wanted. Recall how good you felt about yourself. Tell yourself that you possess the power to bring about any reality you want, and that you are willing to take responsibility for doing so.

Think of the person you have selected. Have you been blaming this person for your relationship not working, or for your life not working? Do you feel like a victim of the other person in any area of your life? If you do not, congratulate yourself for taking responsibility for your life. If you do suffer from any of these issues concerning the relationship, stimulate the hidden point to experience your soul's will to love. Soul link and radiate a forgiving, soft, and consistent love. Lift solar plexus energy into your heart center to surrender negative feelings about the other person. Feel the serenity of love and radiate an accepting love.

You might create a statement to say to yourself that represents your inner strength such as, "I no longer blame you for my unhappiness, or for anything else I have ever blamed you for. I now take responsibility for creating my own happiness." Do not try to change others as a way to make your life work. Join with your soul, affirm your power to create the life and relationships you want, and begin now to take whatever steps are necessary to do so.

Work with and evolve any subpersonalities who feel they do not possess the power to create the relationship you want. Discover if there are any who are afraid to be powerful or do not believe that it is possible to have supportive, loving relationships.

Anytime you catch yourself feeling powerless or like a victim, strengthen your belief that you are the creator of your reality by saying to yourself, "I can choose whatever reality I want. I am choosing to be here and experience this reality." No matter what is happening, how you are being treated, or how powerless you feel to change your relationship, start by telling yourself that you *do* have a choice and this is what you are choosing. Even though you cannot imagine how you might be choosing what you are experiencing, telling yourself this will help you to believe that *you* are the creator of your life. Take time to recognize the decisions you made that created the situation you are in. You do not need others to give you what you want; you and your soul can create any life you can imagine for yourself.

*F*ocus *on what you want rather
than on what you do not want.*

To create what you want in a relationship, you need to
*know* what you want. Most people know what they do not
want, yet find it hard to think of what they do want. Stop
paying attention to or complaining about all the things you
want that you do not have. Do not dwell on past hurts or
remember times when the other person disappointed you;
instead recall times when you felt loved and nurtured. Do not
think about all the things this person is doing that you do not
want this person to do, but reflect instead on all the things
this person does that you love and appreciate. Your thoughts
and actions draw certain behaviors from people. If you
constantly review how others have caused you pain, they will
receive your pictures and live them out by creating more of
the same. Whenever you catch a negative thought, or feel
upset, angry, or distant from someone because this person is
not giving you what you want, change your perspective. Focus
instead on what *is* working in your relationship. Use this to
experience life from your soul's perspective—one that sees
peace, perfection, and beauty; that knows all is well; and that
is certain that the universe is working for you.

Think of the person you have chosen. Pay attention to the
kind of thoughts you have about this relationship. Do you
think of what is wrong between you, or of what the other
person is doing that you do not want him or her to do? To
create the relationship you want, change these thoughts.
Circulate energy among your heart centers and move into a
state of soul love. Feel your connection to all the love in the
universe. From this state of love, think of what you *do want*
in your relationship. For instance, instead of saying, "Do not
ignore me," say instead, "I appreciate when you listen to and
pay attention to me." Acknowledge other people when they

act in ways you like. If you can, state what you want as an essence quality of love, such as, "I want to experience more joy, harmony, love, softness, and so on between us." Radiate that quality to the other person as you soul link.

*View other people's actions as mirrors.*
*Discover what their behaviors*
*are telling you about yourself.*

A very important principle of relationship is that you cannot change another person; you can only transform yourself. You cannot force people to act in certain ways. Punishing, withdrawing, or trying to make people do what you want only strengthens their resistance. It turns your power over to others, making them the source of meeting your needs rather than yourself. You cannot make people change; however you can modify your reaction to their behavior. You can awaken your heart centers and shift your perceptions, beliefs, and thoughts. You can release needing others to alter their behavior, and love and accept them instead. When you work in this way you can feel the greatest power you possess to make your life work—the power to change yourself.

Have you been wanting someone to act in certain ways to please you? Join with your soul to stimulate the hidden point of your solar plexus center, strengthening your will to love. Ask your soul to increase your capacity to love so that you can accept and love this person even if the way you are treated does not change. Lift solar plexus energy into your heart center and surrender your desires or expectations of this person. Let go of any power struggles you might have experienced as you tried to change this person. Ask your soul questions such as, "How can I shift my perception of this person's behavior? How can I react differently?" Let insights and new understandings come into your mind. Soul link and radiate a transparent, amplifying, and accepting love. Decide to change yourself and the way you view this relationship. Feel your soul's power, light, and will flow through you, giving you the strength and courage needed to make changes in yourself and in your life.

Think of a time when you accepted someone's behavior and as a result the love between you increased. Remember the inner peace you felt as you stopped fighting and trying to change the other person. As you alter your response to people's conduct, your relationships will transform. Other people's behavior may change, yet you are not expecting this as a reward for your acceptance and love. As you give up the need for others to modify their behavior, you free them from resisting you, which may make it easier for them to act in more loving ways. Release the need for results. You can only change yourself. As you alter your perceptions and behavior, your relationship will naturally reflect these shifts. You cannot predict the ways in which your relationship or the other person will change, however.

Even if you leave a particular relationship, you will still need to alter your reaction to this kind of behavior, or you will likely encounter more of the same behavior in a new relationship. You need to change the patterns within you that have attracted this type of behavior. You might need to work with your soul so that you can surrender the belief that you are a victim, value yourself more, focus more on the essence rather than the form, and follow the universal laws of relationship. Then you will attract someone who will respond to you in new ways.

## *C*hange your relationships by changing yourself.

One of the principles of relationship is that people mirror for you dramas that are going on within yourself. Other people's behavior toward you reflects something you are doing to yourself. Create the relationship you want by viewing all the things that are happening in your relationship as a mirror for something that is happening within you. You might think that if only the other person acted differently, your relationship would be better. When you learn to see other people's actions as mirrors for something that is going on within you, you can use what is happening between you to learn more about yourself.

People treat you the way you are treating yourself. For instance, if someone is rejecting you, you can explore how, in some way, you are rejecting a part of yourself or your soul. Perhaps you reject your deeper urges or push away your feelings. If someone is putting up walls between you, ask yourself where you are putting up walls in your life. If someone is ignoring, neglecting, or criticizing you, discover the ways you are ignoring, neglecting, or criticizing yourself.

Think about some way another person is treating you that you would like to alter. Blend with your soul and ask yourself, "How is the way this person is treating me mirroring how I am treating myself? How is the attitude or behavior I want the other person to correct something I need to transform in myself?" Thank the other person for providing you with an opportunity to learn more about yourself from being in this situation. Join with your soul and feel its will to love as it activates the hidden point. Lift solar plexus energy into your heart center to release any blame or anger. Soul link and radiate a soft, forgiving love. Resolve to shift the pattern within yourself that this person is mirroring. As you do, you will no longer need the other person to mirror this behavior to you, and this person will be free to act in new ways. If this person's behavior does not change, you will probably choose to spend your time with people who do mirror the new way you are treating yourself.

*Recognize the moment-to-moment*
*choices you are making*
*in a relationship.*

Every moment you are making choices that determine whether or not you are expressing soul love and creating the relationship you want. No choice is too small to make a difference. Loving others starts with bringing more awareness to the choices, actions, and decisions you make on a moment-to-moment basis. Great relationships are not created through one big event. They are built through a series of small daily choices to be kind, to love, and to forgive. Create harmony where there has been disharmony. Use your words to heal and empower others. You can have relationships that bring joy to your heart and a smile to your face. You can experience other people looking at you with love in their eyes. You can create the relationships you want!

# Soul Play

Creating the relationship you want comes from changing yourself. Your outer world is a mirror of your inner world. Choose from the list below one way to change yourself as a step to creating the relationship you want.

1. Think of the soul love quality you want to experience in a relationship. Soul link, and radiate this quality to the other person.

2. If you are experiencing a situation you do not like, affirm that you are choosing this experience, for as you do you are also affirming that you have the power to change it.

3. Focus on what you want rather than on what you do not want in a relationship. Thank and acknowledge the other person for all the ways this person gives love to you.

4. Reflect on one way someone is treating you that you do not like. Discover how this mirrors a way you are treating yourself in some area. Decide to treat yourself differently.

5. If there is any drama occurring between you and another person, ask your soul to help you recognize and change whatever drama this reflects within you.

6. Think about a change you want another person to make. Radiate an accepting love and alter your perception of this person's behavior.

7. Take a moment to acknowledge at least five things that are working in your relationship with someone.

# CHAPTER 17

# Dissolving Obstacles to Love

*You surrender those things that separate you
from your soul's love for yourself and others.
You discover love in every situation.*

As you practice soul love, you are learning a new skill. There will be many times when you remember to express the qualities of soul love, and there will be times when you do not. You may encounter situations with others that you find difficult to accept or love. You may recall a higher way to act, yet still choose to act in old, unloving ways. It is a great challenge to express soul love steadily and consistently. It takes a repeated, continual focus on love to awaken your heart centers.

You do not need to be perfect in expressing soul love. Do not be hard on yourself if you are having a bad day, feel unloving, or are unable to express a quality of soul love in a particular situation. What is important is the direction in which you are progressing. Appreciate yourself every time you express soul love, and forgive yourself every time you do not.

Start dissolving obstacles to love by feeling your soul's love for you. Forgive and love yourself by discovering and releasing any unloving thoughts or feelings you have about yourself. Notice if you are criticizing, judging, or making yourself wrong for who you are. You can only love others as much as you love yourself. Receive your soul's love for you as often as you can remember to do so.

## Bring consciousness to your relationships.

Dissolving obstacles to love requires an awareness of the thoughts, words, and actions you express toward another. Think of the person you selected. How aware are you of the other person—of this person's essence, being, and soul? How aware are you of yourself and your intent to be loving when you are with this person?

To dissolve obstacles to love and create a soul relationship does not require that you bond or be together every moment. It does require that you bring a growing awareness to your interactions with people so you can more consistently express soul love no matter how you feel or how they are acting.

Picture the person you are creating a soul relationship with. What is this person's day like? How aware are you of the reality of this other person? Soul link and connect with this person's soul. Sense reality through this person's eyes. What gift of love could you give this person today? See yourself doing so, bringing more awareness and consciousness to your relationship.

## Think positively of your relationships.

To dissolve obstacles to love, you will want to release criticism and replace it with praise, support, and assistance. An attitude of support assists people in fulfilling their potential. Think of a time you were praised—how good you felt about yourself and how motivated you felt to do even better.

To release criticism of others, first let go of criticizing yourself. Think of something you have been criticizing yourself for. Blend with your soul, aligning your heart center's jewel with your soul's jewel. Breathe in, lifting energy from your heart center up to your head center. Breathe out, sending your soul's will to love to the hidden point of your solar plexus center. Breathe in and lift solar plexus energy into your heart center. Absorb the softness and patience, the peace and serenity of soul love. As you lift solar plexus energy into your heart center, surrender any need to treat yourself in an unloving way. From this space of love, change criticism of yourself in some area into self-appreciation. Think of all the good things you are doing and how much progress you have made in this area.

Think of the person you have chosen to soul link with. Is there anything you have been criticizing this person for? From a state of soul love, create a loving message to convey to the other person your love and support. You might say something mentally such as, "I release my criticism of you. I accept you for who you are. I love, support, and acknowledge the good in you." You might add, "I appreciate and love you for _____." Think of as many things as you can to appreciate about this person. Recognize how far this person has come rather than focusing on how far he or she has to go. Search out the beauty and goodness within this person. Acknowledge how often you do focus on what is good and beautiful in people, and affirm your desire to do this even more frequently.

What if every time you found fault with others, or thought of something they could do better or should be paying attention to, you asked instead, "How does my criticism of other people apply to me?" Even if you think there is no way your observations of others apply to you or your life, be willing to explore how they might. Think of the other person as representing an aspect of yourself. Ask, "Is there anywhere I am doing what I am criticizing the other person for?" Examine your life carefully. The essence of what you criticize another for is usually a quality you are working on developing in yourself. You may have that trait to a lesser degree, or expressed in another way.

Praise and acknowledge people when they demonstrate qualities and behaviors you like. People will often do better at what you praise them for. Honor the light in yourself and in others by thinking and talking positively of your relationships. Emphasize the good, and you will have even more good things come to you.

## *Transform conflict by surrendering to love.*

Even in the best of relationships, you may find yourself experiencing conflict. If you are in the middle of a fight or argument with someone, merge with your soul. Use your inbreath to lift energy from your heart center up to your head center. With your outbreath, join with your soul to send the will to love to activate the hidden point. Imagine that any negative energy within the other person that has stimulated the bright point of your solar plexus center is being absorbed into the hidden point, then lifted into your heart center. If the situation is too intense for you to remember these steps, simply lift solar plexus energy into your heart center over and over until you can feel the serenity of soul love. Rather than thinking of the other person's energy as negative energy, picture it as a gift of pure energy you can circulate among your heart centers to further awaken them. At the soul level there is no good or bad energy. There is simply energy. It is how you use energy that determines its usefulness to you.

You can bring the serenity of love into any area of conflict or disagreement between you and others. Start by joining with your soul to send its will to love into the hidden point. Lift solar plexus energy into your heart center until you can feel the serenity of soul love as you think about this area of conflict. Soul link, sense your soul and the other person's soul, and radiate a serene, accepting, and transparent love. Affirm your desire to interact in a loving way by creating an inner statement to say to yourself that brings you peace, such as, "I release any conflict between us. I open to all the love that is possible. I surrender whatever within myself is standing in the way of our love."

Acknowledge any unloving feelings you have toward the other person. Do not force yourself to feel loving. Keep lifting solar plexus energy into your heart center until you can release any desires to hurt the other through unloving actions or words. Love and evolve any subpersonalities who still feel angry or hurt. Do not dwell on the situation or the outcome. Focus on the light within this person, rather than on any darkness. Become aware of the Universal Presence of Love that encompasses and permeates this situation with love.

*Join with the other person's soul
to dissolve obstacles to love.*

There may come a time in your relationship when you feel stuck or unable to find actions that allow you to express soul love. Start with the understanding that every situation is temporary. Things *will* change. Often you set up situations where there seem to be no solutions so you will be challenged to go to a higher level to find answers, drawing upon inner resources that you did not even know you had. Loving another provides you with many opportunities for growth.

You can move beyond stuck places by waiting for something to happen, or you can work with your soul, awaken your heart centers, and bring soul love into a situation to transform it. Rather than giving up, or feeling locked in a stalemate, blend with your soul. Let energy circulate among your heart centers. Feel your soul's serenity, expand and evolve your love, and align with your soul's will to love. Lift solar plexus energy into your heart center to transform and purify denser energies that may exist between you and the other person.

Soul link, and connect with the other person's soul. Ask your two souls to work together to find a winning solution for both of you. Believe that a winning solution does exist and will appear. If you continue to feel anxiety about the situation, lift solar plexus energy into your heart center over and over until you can feel the serenity of soul love. When you are able, radiate the soul love qualities of harmony, compassion, and patience. Invite the Being of Love into your heart center and radiate this refined love to the other person.

Forgive the other person if you can. Explore how this situation is offering you an opportunity to awaken your heart centers and to grow closer to your soul. Ask how the drama between you is mirroring something that is going on within you. Ask yourself what you might change in yourself to resolve this drama. Trust your soul and the other person's soul to work from a higher level to bring solutions. Take action only when you have a sense of what to do that feels right and loving. Continue to think and speak positively of your relationship and envision the highest and best occurring between you.

*E*xperience the power
*in your ability to be vulnerable.*

To have loving relationships you will need to keep your heart open and be willing to be vulnerable. You do not want to build walls that shut out people. Walls imprison you more than they keep others out. You will have to take down the walls that you put between you and others to have soul relationships, for walls are obstacles to love. Practice keeping your heart open, even when you are in difficult situations. Doing so awakens your heart centers and brings you closer to your soul.

When you are willing to be vulnerable, you have nothing to defend. You do not need to apologize, explain yourself, or put distance between yourself and others. You accept yourself as you are. You do not try to live up to an image of perfection so others will think better of you. You stop feeling inferior or superior to others. You are aware of the strength that comes from letting others see that you are not perfect. You recognize that you are a lovable, worthy, and wonderful person just as you are.

When you are able to be vulnerable, you let go of pride so you can create more love between yourself and others. If someone seems hurt or angry with you, you heal the relationship by asking yourself and the other person how you might change the way you offer love. You are willing to look at yourself honestly, admit when you have been unloving, and extend an offer of peace. You examine what thoughts, beliefs, and feelings separate you from others, and you are willing to change them. You are secure enough within yourself to know that it is all right not to be perfect and loving all the time. You can forgive and accept yourself, and thus be more open and vulnerable with others. You can support and encourage others in being more open and vulnerable with you. Think of times when people let down their defenses, or let go of their pride, and built bridges rather than walls. You probably felt very loving and accepting of people when they were willing to be vulnerable. Recall a time when you were vulnerable, and someone was loving and understanding with you.

Bring to mind the person you have chosen. Identify an area where you have put up a wall between you, thinking that you would not be loved if you were to reveal your true self in this area. You may be protecting yourself, or trying to live out an image that you think will make you seem more worthy or lovable. Or, perhaps the other person is upset with you, and you need to be more open to hearing the other person's complaints so you can modify your behavior and heal the relationship.

As you think of this area or situation where you have put up walls between you and another, circulate energy among your heart centers. See yourself becoming soft and vulnerable, with nothing to defend. You have compassion for yourself, as well as for the other person. Picture letting down your defenses, and being willing to be seen for who you are. Create a statement you can repeat to yourself that reflects this decision. You might say, "I offer you love that is trusting, open, and vulnerable. I am willing for you to see me as I really am."

Ask your soul to assist you in letting down the walls you may have built around your heart in this area. You might make a symbol of a wall around your heart center, and imagine your soul radiating love that melts or dissolves this wall. In addition, if it applies, you might say to the other person, "I want to know how I can love you in ways that are pleasing to you. I am open to hearing how I might better express love to you."

As you stay open and vulnerable, not needing to defend or protect yourself, you can dissolve obstacles to love. It does not matter how the other person acts, or whether or not this person accepts you when you are humble and vulnerable. You have affirmed your worth, you have allowed yourself to be seen for who you are, and you have taken down the walls around your heart that keep you from expressing soul love and awakening your heart centers.

# Release the need to save people.

You can dissolve obstacles to love by releasing the need to save people from their problems. You can love others as your soul does by allowing them to be responsible for their own lives. Taking care of others, worrying about their lives, and solving their problems can occupy so much of your attention and emotions that you have no energy left to put into your own life and spiritual path. When you stop saving others, you can release any resentment you might feel for all the time and energy you spent on them. When you save others, you can become a victim when they do not use your help in the way you would like, when they continue to create similar problems, or when they expect and demand that you continue to save them.

Learn to recognize when you are helping others because you feel that they do not have the strength or ability to solve their own problems. When you feel an urge to help people in a way that will "save" them or take away their lessons, stop! You may find that your desire to help others really comes from your own need to feel better and to have less concern and worry about their problems. Assume that people have the ability to solve their own problems, even if you cannot see how they will. While your soul is interested in assisting people, it does not interfere with their lives. It allows people to have their own ideas, to live in whatever way they choose, to learn from their mistakes, and to achieve their own successes.

Your soul knows that taking responsibility for themselves and their lives is one of the most important ways people can grow and become strong. It knows that people have worked hard to bring about their current circumstances, no matter how difficult or unpleasant, so they can learn and grow. Experiencing the consequences of their actions provides people with the motivation to make changes in their lives. Saving people makes them weaker rather than stronger.

It is more important to give people tools that assist them in making their lives work than to save them from the specific problems they have created. If you are not certain if you are rescuing people or empowering them with your aid, ask yourself if your assistance is giving them tools to change their lives or simply bailing them out of a reoccurring problem. Are they working to change themselves and the thoughts and beliefs that created their current condition, or are they playing the victim, hoping that you or others will fix the problems they have created? When people play the victim and expect others to assist them, yet take no action to empower themselves, helping them is usually saving them. When people are striving to lift themselves out of their current condition and taking responsibility for having created their challenges, your aid is usually empowering.

Think of the person you have chosen. Blend with your soul and ask it to show you if there is anywhere you are taking away this person's lessons, solving this person's problems, or taking too much responsibility for this person's life. Soul link and radiate a transparent love. Circulate energy among your heart centers, paying attention to lifting solar plexus energy into your heart center. Create a statement that will act as a guideline for how you intend to express love, such as, "I relinquish the need to save you. I turn the responsibility for your life over to you and your soul. I do this as an affirmation that you have all the inner strength, resources, and wisdom within you to solve your own problems." Experience your soul's serene love, a love that does not need to *do* anything. Release any desires you have for this person, allowing this person to do whatever he or she chooses. Recall a time when you refused to save someone and that person did just fine without your help. If you still feel tempted to save someone, or are not certain if your assistance would make this person weaker or stronger, blend with your soul and ask it to show you what it would do in this situation.

## $A$ssist others by offering soul love.

When you perceive that people are in trouble, hurting, or facing life-threatening or desperate situations, the most important work you can do for them is your soul work. To assist people in these situations, soul link and radiate love. Ask for these people's guardian angel, soul, or the Being of Love to assist them. If they are stuck in a seemingly hopeless or desperate situation, be inventive and broadcast an image of something such as a doorway, a path of light that they might find, or other images that could assist these people. Surround them with love and light. Affirm that they have all the power, wisdom, and strength to handle whatever circumstances they have created or found themselves in.

Refusing to take outer actions to save others or to bail them out of the problems they have caused may seem unloving. Soul love is not always soft and accommodating. Sometimes the highest action you can take involves being firm rather than giving in, or allowing others to find their own solutions rather than solving or taking away their problems. Even though their personality might not thank or appreciate you for letting them suffer the consequences of their actions, their soul will rejoice at their opportunity to grow from the situations they have brought into their lives. When you refuse to save people and radiate love instead, you allow people to gain the confidence, personal power, and inner strength that come from solving their own problems.

If, after all your inner work you feel a strong urge to take action, do so. Your action will now come from your soul connection, and will be a soul urge rather than a personality reaction to save or take away someone's lessons. While your soul does not save others, it is always working with other people's soul to empower them to raise their consciousness, to find and follow their higher path, to become a more perfect light, and to serve others.

# SOUL PLAY

Think of someone with whom you would like to evolve your relationship through dissolving obstacles to love. Blend with your soul, soul link, and follow one or more of these suggestions:

1. Bring more consciousness to your relationship. For the next few hours or days, notice if the thoughts you have about your relationship and the choices you are making reflect the reality you want to create. Are they positive, supportive, and loving?

2. Mentally or verbally tell the other person some of the things you love and appreciate about this person.

3. Think of something you are criticizing another person for. Ask yourself, "How does my criticism of the other person apply to me or my life?"

4. Transform conflict by stimulating the hidden point with your soul's will to love, and lifting solar plexus energy into your heart center. Soul link and ask both of your souls to find a winning solution.

5. If there is anywhere you have put up a wall between you and another, imagine your soul radiating love that melts or dissolves this wall.

6. Be vulnerable and ask someone you love, "How can I love you in ways that are pleasing to you? I am open to hearing how I might better express love to you."

7. Before you assist another person, ask yourself if you are empowering this person to become wiser and stronger, or if you are attempting to save this person from the consequences of his or her actions. Then, soul link and radiate soul love.

# CHAPTER 18

# Exploring New Ways to Love

*You deepen your relationship to your soul
and connect more deeply with the soul of others.
You find and follow the path of love
that is uniquely yours.*

As you awaken your heart centers and soul link, you will experience new insights, perspectives, and feelings about your relationships. Your vision of what you want in relationships may change. Old ways of relating to people that worked for you in the past may not seem right for who you are becoming. What you want out of a relationship may be shifting as you change what you value, and expand your goals and dreams. You may experience an increasing desire for soul contact. You may want to spend time with people in new and different ways. Now that you have created a vision of your relationships, learned the universal laws of relationships, and dissolved obstacles to love, you are ready to discover new ways to love yourself and others.

As you awaken your heart centers you become aware that there is a "right relationship" to have with everyone in your life. Imagine all the relationships in your life working and providing you with an opportunity to love as your soul. Right relationship is established first at the soul level, through soul-to-soul contact. After you work at the soul level, you can find new ways to be together that support you in expressing soul love and in fulfilling the higher purposes of your relationship.

*Walk on your own path.*
*Release any paths*
*that are not yours to follow.*

An important step to take in opening to new ways to love, and in releasing old ways, is to explore the relationship patterns you learned from your parents. You can let go of those ways of relating to others that do not serve you. Some of your parents' patterns and the ways they lived their lives are very valuable, and you will want to claim them as your own. Some of their patterns do not fit who you are, and do not allow you to express the love that is awakening within you. You can release any relationship habits, patterns, visions, and goals you learned from your parents that do not fit you, and choose your own way of being. You can relate to others in new ways that are different from your parents' ways of relating to each other and to other people.

Because of deep loyalty to and love for your parents (even if you outwardly rebelled against or resisted your parents), many of you have not allowed yourselves to have better lives or relationships than your parents. You may have unconsciously limited how much joy, love, success, or abundance you have allowed yourself to have. Or, you may be living out some of your parents' dreams and desires for their lives or for your life that are not your own desires or your soul's path for you.

You can experience more love, joy, and aliveness than your parents. You can have better relationships, a more open heart, and a different spiritual path than your parents. To start, blend with your soul. Circulate energy and light among your heart centers and move into a state of soul love. Breathe in and lift energy from your heart to your head center, feeling the serenity of soul love and expanding into the oneness of love. Breathe out and join with your soul to send light from your head center to stimulate the hidden point, increasing your will to love yourself. Breathe in and lift solar plexus energy into your heart center. Surrender the desires and expectations others have for your life that you do not want to follow.

From this state of wisdom, expansion, serenity, and love, soul link with your mother. It does not matter whether or not you know her, or whether or not she is alive. You can work with your birth mother or any other important woman who was a role model for you. Thank her for all the gifts you have received.

Picture yourself as a small child walking on a path of light, hand in hand with this woman. Sense, at a certain point, your joint path becoming two paths. You are walking on your own path of light, separate from her path. You bring with you all the gifts you want to keep and all the love you have received. You relinquish all the habits and patterns that are not on your path of love. A warm sun is at the end of your path, much like the sun at sunset. As you continue on your path, this sun amplifies all the qualities that are your soul qualities, visions, dreams, and path. It assists you in releasing anything that does not belong with you on your path. See your mother following her path into the light. Your two paths may be side by side, or they may go in different directions. You are now walking firmly on your own path, headed toward the light.

After you finish this process with your mother, repeat it with your father, or any important male role model. Thank him for all the gifts you have received from him and all the love that was given to you. Release any of your father's dreams, goals, and personality patterns that you do not want to claim as your own. Follow the path of love that is uniquely yours. See yourself walking on your own path toward the light.

# *B*ecome aware
## *of your soul's rhythm.*
## *Cultivate time alone.*

You can discover new ways to love by exploring how much time you want to spend with others, and how much time you want to spend by yourself. As you grow closer to your soul, the amount of time you want to spend with people may change. You may find yourself valuing time alone to recharge, to meditate, to connect with your soul, and to simply be. It is important to spend time alone to hear your inner self and to feel balanced. Do not make yourself wrong, or tell yourself that something is wrong with your relationships, if you want to spend more time alone. Think of an occasion when you spent time alone, simply being quiet. Remember how good you felt. It is in moments of silence, when you are alone, that your soul can best work with you to send you energy and ideas.

Some people may feel threatened if you want time to be alone or to do things that do not involve them. You may feel disloyal and guilty for wanting more time for yourself. Spouses, children, and friends can have many expectations of how much time they want you to spend with them. Stop feeling that you must fulfill other people's pictures of how much time you owe them. You can love in new ways by giving yourself permission to take all the time you need to be by yourself.

Imagine that you have a reservoir of energy. Picture a gauge that reads from empty to full. Close your eyes for a moment, and see what the gauge on your reservoir of energy reads. Ask your soul to show you what you could do to fill up so you have more energy. How much time alone would recharge you? What could you do with your time that would allow you to flourish and feel revitalized? Think of a time when you did nourish and take care of yourself. Recall how much more love and energy you had to give others afterward. Recognize that when you take care of yourself, you offer others a gift—the present of a relaxed, revitalized, and energized self.

Soul link with the person you have picked. Mentally give your thanks in advance to this person for giving you freedom to do whatever you want with your time. You might mentally say, "Thank you for giving me the time and space to do what I need to feel balanced, to connect with my soul, to recharge myself, and to experience my own rhythm and path." Pay attention to your impulses to be alone, for these can be times when your soul is calling to you to receive its light, joy, will, presence, power, love, or any of its qualities that will enhance your life.

Work with any subpersonality who is afraid you might lose this person's love if you take time to be by yourself. Spending time alone, doing the things you love, and experiencing your soul can assist you in connecting with the oneness and in creating more harmony between yourself and the universe. Even if you have young children, it is important to take time alone to recharge yourself. Soul link with your children's souls, and thank them for allowing you to take time to be by yourself. Think of ways your children could be cared for while you take the time you need. When your reservoir is full you have more light, love, and energy to offer them.

Give other people permission to do whatever they want to do with their time and life. Make a statement to yourself to remember to act in this way. You might say something such as, "I give all the people in my life permission to live in their soul's rhythm and to do whatever they need to do to feel balanced and to recharge themselves." Evolve and love any subpersonalities who might resist giving others the freedom to do what they want. Talk to and evolve any who feel that people might leave, pull away, or take advantage if you give them too much freedom. People will love you more, not less, when you do.

*H*old high, positive images of yourself.
Ask others to do the same.

Explore new ways to love through changing the images you hold of loved ones, and working with them to alter the images they hold of you. Through holding high, positive images and thoughts of one another, you can let go of old ways of relating that may be holding you back, and find new ways to be together.

Relationships can become less alive when people hold outdated pictures and images of each other based on who they used to be rather than on who they have become. You may want to distance yourself from someone because you have evolved and grown, yet the other person has not recognized or acknowledged the changes you have made. When friends, parents, children, spouses, and other loved ones think of you as you used to be, rather than who you are now, it can be harder to act in new ways. People give you a wonderful gift of love when they hold a high vision of you, believing in you and your potential even if you have not yet manifested it.

Reflect on the vision the person you have selected has of you. Does this person hold a high vision of you? Does this person believe in your potential, or remind you instead of your faults? Do you like the self this person reflects back to you? If not, update your self-image. Before others can hold a positive image of you, you will need to have positive images of yourself.

Feel your soul's presence. Think of an area of your life where the other person is reflecting back to you a negative image, or holding onto an old perception of who you used to be. Make a picture in your mind of the image you want the other person to hold of you in this area. Soul link and broadcast to the other person your new self-image in this area. You can do this when you are meditating or when you are in physical contact with this person. If you catch this person speaking or acting in ways that reflect a perception of you that does not fit who you are, soul link and broadcast the picture you want this person to have of you in this area. As you soul link, imagine the Solar Light and the light of your soul dissolving any negative or outdated images the other person is sending you about yourself. The other person may or may not alter his or her notions of you as you do this. However, the most important thing you are doing is steadily holding a positive image of yourself. You will want to live out this new image with your actions and words, and not revert back to old behaviors that reinforce the other person's outdated perceptions of you.

## *Recognize the potential for greatness in yourself and others.*

You may need to update the images you hold of loved ones. Think of the person with whom you have been soul linking. Are you holding any outdated pictures of this person that you need to update? Identify at least one area where you might be holding a less evolved picture of this person. Think of a new vision you could hold for this person. Soul link and broadcast your updated image to this person. You might say mentally something such as, "I now see you as _____, and I will hold this positive vision of you to assist you in growing and evolving." Make a commitment to identify and transform other negative pictures you are holding of this person.

Go beyond updating the images you hold of others and recognize the greatness that lies within people. Start by identifying the greatness that lies within yourself. Join with your soul and sense its beauty and light. Reflect on all the wonderful soul qualities you already express. Review your life, noting how you have always felt that there was something special you came to do. You know that there are seeds of greatness within you, just waiting for the right conditions to emerge. Reflect on how at every moment you are becoming a more beautiful and perfect light.

Think of and soul link with the person you have selected. Invite the Being of Love into your heart center to assist you in seeing the highest and best in this person. Picture the Solar Light above both of you, assisting you in sensing or seeing more clearly some of the greatness that lies within this person. Imagine that anything that hides the light of this person's soul is falling away, until its radiant light shines through at every level. Sense the potential for love within this person, even if this person is not yet able to express love consistently. Ask your soul to show you some of the soul qualities this person has within as seeds of light waiting to emerge. Focus on these gems of light, paying no attention to any darkness you sense. Remember how when you were first together you recognized this person's potential and greatness. Notice how updating the image you hold of this person opens and expands the energy between you as you focus on this person's potential and greatness.

You might strengthen your decision to recognize what is good and beautiful about the person you have chosen by affirming to yourself, "I love and recognize the greatness within you, and I also love those parts of you that are not yet evolved." Acknowledge that there is a beautiful side to this person, even if you are in the middle of a disagreement, or if the person seems to be in a bad mood or nonreceptive.

Focusing on what is good about people will assist them in manifesting and bringing those qualities into their lives. You may find people acting in more loving ways when you recognize all the good and light within them. As you see the light within others, you assist them in knowing and expressing this light.

## Commit to your spiritual growth.

Commit to your growth and spiritual evolution as a way to increase your self-love and to have more love to offer others. As you grow you have more to offer your relationships. You are able to take the actions and do the things that make your relationships successful. You are focused on higher purpose, your vision expands, and you have beliefs that support the success of your relationships.

When you make a commitment to your spiritual growth, you steadily gain more faith and trust in yourself, in your ability to set boundaries, and in your capacity to radiate a consistent, steady love. When you are committed to your aliveness, you do not fear that a relationship will stop you from growing, expanding, and fulfilling your higher path and purpose. You see your relationships as a part of your higher path, as making a contribution to your aliveness, and as offering you an opportunity to grow through learning how to love.

Connect with your soul often, and let it show you what you might do to grow spiritually. Believe that spending time to meditate, to connect with your soul, to transform your subpersonalities, to awaken your heart centers, and to do inner work is some of the most valuable time you can spend. Turn your daily activities into your spiritual practice of expressing love.

## Mentally say to loved ones, "I support your becoming enlightened."

It is important to support other people's growth. As people grow spiritually, they will be able to love you in new and higher ways, although you are not supporting their growth for this reason. Think of the person you have selected. Circulate light among your heart centers and move into a state of soul love. Extend your unconditional support for the other person's growth, success, and enlightenment. From the bottom of your heart, want this loved one to be happy, fulfilled, and successful. Take a moment to picture this person becoming enlightened. Let a mental message go out from you to this person that says, "I support your becoming enlightened with all my heart." Work with any of your subpersonalities who might be afraid that if the other person were happy and fulfilled, he or she would no longer love or want you. One of the greatest gifts you can give others is to hold a vision of their becoming enlightened.

## *Study and learn relationship skills.*

Take time to create better relationships by learning practical relationship skills. Discover new ways to love by listening to tapes, reading books, watching videos, or taking classes. Relationships offer you an opportunity to open your heart. Nurture and cultivate your relationships so they can mirror the soul love within you. Honor your relationships as a path of enlightenment and as a vehicle for awakening your heart centers.

# Soul Play

Blend with your soul and choose one new way to love yourself or another from the list below. Or, be creative and think of additional new ways to love yourself and someone else.

1. Think of one relationship pattern your mother or father had. Decide if you want to have this pattern. If not, work with your soul to release it.

2. Look with your inner eyes at the gauge on your reservoir of energy. How full is it? Get quiet and ask your soul to give you ideas about how to recharge yourself.

3. Ask your soul to show you how often it would like you to blend with it so you can receive all the gifts it wants to give you. How much contact does your soul want from you in the next day, week, and month?

4. Think of an image you would like a loved one to have of you. Hold this image steadily as you soul link and broadcast it to this person.

5. Think of a new, positive image you could hold of a loved one. Broadcast this image to this person as you soul link.

6. Recognize the potential for greatness within another. See the radiance of this person's soul shining through anything that veils this person's light.

7. Mentally or verbally say to a loved one, "I support your becoming enlightened with all my heart." Send this same thought to a complete stranger today.

8. Say, "I support my becoming enlightened with all of my being." Commit to your spiritual growth as a way to have more love to offer others.

## Chapter 19

# Changing or Releasing a Relationship

*Your soul magnetizes. Your soul sends away.*
*All that is good and beautiful grows.*
*All that no longer serves the soul is released.*

As your contact with your soul deepens and your heart centers awaken, you may find your life changing. Old issues from the past or relationship patterns may surface for you to examine. Your expanding love and changing self-image may make you feel less content with current situations, relationships, or the way certain people treat you. As you surrender those attitudes, thoughts, beliefs, and energies that stand in the way of love, what you want in a relationship can change. This can be a time of leaving the past and what you have created, for your soul will fill you with new visions and dreams, new goals and aspirations.

As you grow spiritually, your relationships may change in ways that support you. People may evolve with you. Or, people may not grow in the same way you are growing. They may still be expanding, yet growing in different directions than you, or at a different pace.

As your heart centers awaken, you begin to heal the places within you that have felt unloved and unacceptable. When you feel more whole and complete, you want relationships that are loving and supportive and that enrich and nourish you. You want to be treated in ways that honor you. You refuse to be part of any drama that makes you feel less than others, sorry for yourself, or a victim. You do not want these feelings, and you stop putting yourself in situations that create them. You no longer want to be around people whose lives are not working or who try to draw you into their constant dilemmas and dramas. You no longer want to be around people who constantly complain about their lives yet take no action to solve their problems. Instead you want to be around people whose lives are working, who are making a contribution, and who are growing and making soul contact.

Sometimes you want to change your relationship with someone, or leave a relationship because you have learned everything you came together to learn. You may have fulfilled your higher purpose in being together. Sometimes you need to release people because they are harmful to you in some way. You may need to create more distance, or not be around certain people physically. You may be ready to let go of old forms that no longer work for you, and find a new form for your relationship that allows both of you to continue to grow, to fulfill your higher purpose, and to express more love.

*Honor your soul connection no matter*
*what happens to the outer form*
*of your relationship.*

Before you release, change the form, or decrease your involvement with someone, join with your soul and connect with the other person's soul. Commit to honoring the beauty and strength of your soul connection regardless of what changes in the outer form of your relationship. If you are deciding whether or not to change or release a relationship with someone, think of this person now. Blend with your soul and soul link with this person. The most important relationship you have with this person is with his or her soul. Harmonize with the other person's soul and radiate soul love. Affirm your commitment to honoring your soul connection no matter what the outer form of your relationship. Mentally say to the other person, "I commit to having a soul relationship throughout any changes in the outer form of our relationship."

## *Release forms*
### *that no longer serve you.*

Your soul is magnetic. It can be transparent and let energies pass right through it. Your soul can also reject energies that it does not want. It is able to repel energies that are not appropriate, such as those that mask or take away its light. Reflect on the way a magnet works. One end is magnetic to certain energies. The other end repels or pushes away certain energies.

You may know people who have not yet developed the ability to send away or rebuff those energies that do not fit their essence. They may choose relationships with strong-willed people who seem to run their lives. Do not blame or criticize these people for being victims, unable to set boundaries, or having no will of their own. They may seem incapable of protecting themselves or their loved ones. Realize that an important soul lesson they are learning is how to repel and to not be receptive to certain energies. Sometimes people attract relationships with those who seem to take over their lives so they can learn and become strong as they are challenged to set boundaries. You can assist them most by steadily focusing on the essence of their being and the light within them. This assists them in sensing their essence themselves. Hold a clear vision that they will learn how to reject and send away those energies that hide or dampen their light. Accept and love them rather than condemn or blame them for being weak. Feel the serenity of soul love and radiate an accepting, soft, and transparent love.

Strengthen your own ability to reject and release energies that do not fit who you are by blending with your soul. Feel your heart center's jewel aligning with your soul's jewel. Recall how you blended with your soul and your heart center became magnetic with your soul's love. This time, imagine your soul is working in a different way. Your soul is changing its magnetism, so that it sends away those energies that are not appropriate for it. From the center of love within your heart, your soul repels energies that are denser or lower than your vibration. Imagine releasing from yourself those energies you have accepted from the universe that are no longer appropriate for you. You can sense energy leaving at any level—physical, emotional, or mental. Any patterns, habits, or energies you have accepted from others that do not fit you are being released by your soul.

Think of the person with whom you have been creating a soul relationship. Ask your soul to assist you in releasing whatever energy you have taken on from this person that does not fit you. Your soul knows exactly what energies to accept, be transparent to, or to send away. It is always becoming a more beautiful and perfect light. Blend with your soul and let it send away those energies you have accepted from this person that are not appropriate for you, such as certain thoughts, feelings, or beliefs. Soul link, and sense the pure light of soul love that now exists between you.

Next, repeat this process with someone with whom you would like to change the form of your relationship. As you release those energies that do not fit you, you may need to create more distance, stop seeing each other altogether, or only be together at certain times to accomplish specific goals. As you work at this inner level to release those energies between you that no longer reflect who you are, the outer forms and expressions of your relationship will change. Remember to love the other person's soul no matter what changes about your relationship.

*D*iscover if changing your life
will improve your relationship.

Before you end or change the form of a relationship, examine whether you are doing so because the relationship is not working, or because your own life is not working. Sometimes people want to leave an intimate relationship because there is too much stress in their lives, and leaving the relationship seems to be the only way out of a life that is not working. Sometimes people leave a relationship because they feel their life is dull, or because they no longer feel alive. Look within and ask yourself, "If I were happy with my life, or, if I had a less stressful, more joyful life, would I still want to leave this relationship?"

Sometimes people want to withdraw from a relationship because they know of no other way to set limits and boundaries. They feel that to have freedom from another person's expectations and demands, they need to leave the relationship. Ask yourself, "If I could set limits and stop feeling as if I have to fulfill this person's expectations of me, would I still want to leave this relationship?" As you learn to set limits and honor yourself and your needs, you may find that you enjoy being with this person again.

## Decide whether or not to change the form of your relationship.

As you work with your soul to release those energies that do not fit you, you may be trying to decide if you should leave a relationship completely, partially withdraw, or stay and make changes. Do not judge yourself negatively if you cannot make up your mind. Leaving or making changes can be a big decision in an intimate, long-term relationship, especially when your choice impacts many lives. Some people stay in relationships long after the essence of love is gone because they feel that they do not have good enough reasons to leave. Or, they feel they they do not have the inner or outer resources to leave. Sometimes people stay because they are afraid of being alone or of hurting the other person.

Perhaps you are going back and forth, exhausting yourself trying to decide if you should stay in a relationship or end it. If so, spend time in a state of soul love, soul linking with the other person's soul. Review your higher purposes for being in this relationship, and decide if you have fulfilled them. Ask if there is anything you still need to be together to create or finish. Ask your soul to show you if it is part of your higher path to stay in this relationship. Or, ask to know if your relationship is complete and it is time to alter its form. You may not, in fact you probably will not, receive immediate answers. However, through your dreams, feelings, and any events that unfold, you will begin to know more about the changes you need to make. You might make a commitment to staying in and working on your relationship as a way to discover if this path is still possible. Work with those beliefs or patterns that may be holding you back from having a loving relationship. Give yourself a few months or so for things to change before you question leaving or staying again. Release the inner battle with yourself, and decide to make your final decision later. As you live out the decision to stay, at some point you will know if this choice is your highest path and soul's desire.

### *Do not feel you need a reason to change the form of a relationship.*

Many people stay in a relationship, or wait to make changes, until they can find good enough reasons for doing so. You do not need to justify leaving, taking more time for yourself, or changing the form of a relationship. In fact, it is better that you do not have a reason that you give others if the explanation is that you feel the other person has failed you in some way. That could give both of you a sense of failure. Instead, view any changes as your soul does, acknowledging that you have been successful in accomplishing what you came together to learn, that you have fulfilled your higher purpose in being together, and that it is now time to embark upon a new path and find the new forms that will work for both of you.

If you sense that this relationship is complete for you in its current form, make a statement to yourself of how you want to view your transition. You might say, "I release our relationship with love. I will view our relationship as successful and as having fulfilled its purpose." Think of how you have become more loving to yourself and others since you started this relationship. Reflect on all that you have learned and how much you have grown.

View your relationship as a success and keep this in mind throughout all changes, so that you can feel successful as you make the transition in the form of your relationship. Some people believe that success means being together forever, and feel like failures if a relationship ends or changes in form. You may want to redefine what success is for you, such as successfully raising a family, succeeding in what you set out to do, learning what you came together to learn, evolving spiritually in some area, and so on. View all your relationships as successful, even those you have left. You are changing the form of your relationship because it feels right, because you know the time has come, and because you know deep within that it is the best thing to do.

*Receive your soul's strength
and courage as you change
the form of a relationship.*

Sometimes you know it is time to leave or change the form of a relationship, yet you cannot find the inner strength or courage to do so. You may feel the other person depends on you and will not be able to cope or survive without you. You may feel a deep loyalty, even though the relationship has been hard for you or does not honor who you are. You may fear being by yourself and feel that any relationship is better than none. You may lack the resources to leave, or fear the reaction of the other person if you leave. Your partner, spouse, or friend may be a wonderful person, and you do not want to hurt this person by leaving. You may feel that the other person will be mad at you, or even hurt you if you leave, pull away, or change the form of your relationship.

Start by looking at the reasons you are afraid to leave or change this relationship. Take one reason, and write it down.

Turn this into a positive statement. For instance, if you say, "I am afraid to leave or change this relationship because it might hurt the other person," instead say, "I trust that doing the things that are in my highest interests also creates the highest good for the other person." Replace any fears that you are a bad person for honoring your soul and your own needs with thoughts that you are following your deepest wisdom, and in doing so you will provide the other person with an opportunity to grow and evolve.

Some common fears that people have about leaving or changing the form of a relationship are: fear that they will lose the other person completely, fear that they will not find anyone better to love, fear of being alone, fear that no one will love them, fear that they will have no money, and fear that the other person will not be able to survive without them. You may be waiting and hoping for the other person to change, living on your dreams of what the relationship could be rather than facing what the relationship actually is for you. Take time to recognize your fears. Write out a positive statement that you say over and over to yourself to affirm that you have the power to create what you want. As you affirm this, you will have more courage to take the steps you need to take.

You may feel that the other person will not let you leave or change the form of your relationship. You may fear that the consequences of leaving would be too hard to live with. If this is so, join with the other person's soul and ask both of your souls to assist you in leaving or in making the changes you need to make. If you are in an intimate relationship with someone who is angry or abusive, lift solar plexus energy into your heart center until you can feel and radiate the serenity of love. Refuse to be a victim. Be compassionate with yourself. Your life is as important as the other person's. Tell yourself that you *can* live in a nurturing, supportive environment with people who love and respect you. Affirm your freedom by saying to yourself, "I am free. I will do what is the highest and best for myself and my life." If you feel you do not have the resources you need to leave or to change the form of your relationship, call upon the power of your soul often. Ask your soul to work with you to create the resources you need, such as counseling, people to assist you, a job, financial assistance, and whatever you need.

> *A*sk *your soul to assist you*
> *in releasing a relationship*
> *in a loving and harmonious way.*

If you have decided to leave or to change the form of a relationship, work at a soul level with the other person. Just as you pictured with your parents, imagine that you have been walking together on a path of light with this person, and now your two paths are separating. The Solar Light is above both of you. Each of you is becoming a more beautiful and perfect light at every moment, and it is now necessary for you to walk on different paths to continue to grow and evolve into more light. Look at your two paths. How do you picture your paths as you separate from each other? For example, do your paths follow each other for a distance, then go in different directions?

Leaving or changing the form of a relationship can be a challenging time. Have the intent to say and think good things about the other person. If the other person is trying to make you feel guilty, or if you are experiencing negative emotions that you want to transform, lift solar plexus energy into your heart center. Do this anytime you feel you are reacting to unevolved solar plexus energy in yourself or in the other person. Remember, you are decreasing or changing your involvement at the personality level. You can still love this person's soul. Ask both of your souls to assist you so that changes in your relationship can occur in the most harmonious, loving, and balanced way. Picture an easy parting or transition. Think of the relationship as a success. Reflect on all you have accomplished, learned, and created together, and upon your increased capacity to love yourself and others.

## *Forgive those who leave you.*

Sometimes you will alter the form of a relationship by being with someone who leaves you or sees you less often. As you grow and change, people will react in different ways. Some will rejoice with you at your increased light and inner strength. Some will not notice, or it will not make a difference to them. Some may feel threatened and try to control you to keep you from changing. Some people may pull away because they are not ready to match you as your love becomes higher, clearer, and more balanced. They may still need to be in a relationship that involves the kind of lessons you were learning together before you changed. If this is so, they will most likely leave the relationship. They may even find someone else to be with who will repeat the relationship patterns they had with you. This person can teach them what you can no longer teach them, because you have already learned these lessons.

If someone is leaving or has left you, is pulling away from you, acting indifferent, or rejecting you, do not dwell on what you could say or do to draw this person closer again. Reflect on how the other person's actions are mirroring something that is going on within you. Ask how you have been leaving this relationship yourself. Perhaps you have not been emotionally available or have been physically absent for periods of time. You have probably had many doubts about the relationship, or have been receiving inner messages to change or leave the relationship that you have not acted on.

To heal the pain of being left or of leaving a relationship, and to work with this pain as an opportunity to awaken your heart centers, blend with your soul. Lift any hurt feelings from your solar plexus center into your heart center to be healed and released. Invite the Being of Love into your heart center's jewel to assist you. Let the pain dissolve into light that opens the petals of your heart center even more. Affirm that you are a lovable, worthy person and that there is nothing wrong with you that caused this separation.

Even if you cannot imagine how, the other person's leaving might be the best thing that could happen to both of you. It can create the circumstances that allow you to love this person more easily as you relate in new ways. It is freeing you to create a relationship with someone new who will match you at your new level. It gives you more time to put into your own life and to know your soul. Remember and affirm that nothing ever leaves unless something better is coming. You have all that you need within you to create wonderful, loving soul relationships.

# Changing or Releasing a Relationship

# SOUL PLAY

From the list below, pick an activity to work with to change or release a relationship in a loving way.

1. Mentally say to this person's soul, "I commit to maintaining a soul relationship with you throughout any changes in the outer form of our relationship."

2. Ask your soul to reveal more about the changes you need to make to be in right relationship with one another. Do you need to make simple changes, end your outer connection completely, or do something in-between?

3. Ponder this: "If I were excited and happy about my life, would I still want to change or leave this relationship?"

4. If you have been waiting to create a good enough reason to leave or change the relationship, affirm that you can leave or make changes without needing to justify your decision or to have a reason.

5. Reflect on how you have succeeded in doing what you came together to create and accomplish. View your relationship as successful.

6. If you are leaving or changing a relationship, ask your soul to assist you in doing so in a loving, peaceful, and harmonious way. Make a mental picture that changes will happen in a peaceful way.

7. If someone has left or is pulling away from you, and if you are feeling anger or pain, lift these feelings from your solar plexus center into your heart center to be healed and released.

# SECTION IV

# Receiving and Radiating Love

*You join in a celebration of love*
*to call the Great Ones to awaken*
*the heart centers of humanity.*
*You receive and radiate their love.*
*You make wheels of love*
*to bring higher purpose and harmony*
*to your relationships with*
*family, friends, and groups.*
*You join the Beings of Light*
*to radiate love to people in need.*
*Self-love, soul love, group love,*
*love of humanity, and love of life*
*in all dimensions prevail.*

# CHAPTER 20

# A Celebration of Love

*You gather with a group*
*to call the beneficent forces of the Great Ones*
*to awaken the heart centers of humanity.*

Many of you have wondered how you can assist humanity with the vast challenges it is facing. Sometimes these challenges can seem overwhelming and too large for one person to make a difference. Yet, there is something important you can do—something that works and makes a difference: You can join with others to call upon the Great Ones to ask them to send their love and assistance to humanity. You can receive the love of the Great Ones and become a point of light through which their love can flow out to humanity. You can radiate love to friends, loved ones, acquaintances, and groups of people. You can teach love to children. You can be an example of love in your words, actions, and deeds.

Those whom I call the Great Ones include the Masters, Beings of Light, Enlightened Ones, and Beings who are even higher. When enough people desire the evolution of humanity and call upon them for assistance, the Great Ones feel the impact of this call and respond. The Great Ones are so powerful that one moment of their energy can assist in bringing about changes of great magnitude. They can stimulate and

speed up the evolution of humanity through their transmissions of love, light, and energy. The Great Ones send energy
to elevate humanity whenever people are ready for their
assistance and can use it for their evolution. When people join
together to call upon them for the good of humanity rather
than for their own personal gain, the Great Ones can create
enormous good. Because you always have free will, the Great
Ones cannot do anything *for* you; you need to choose to use
the energy you receive from them to bring about changes.

## Join the celebration of love on the soul plane.

In the ceremony that follows, which I will call a *celebration
of love*, you will join with the souls of others to call upon the
Great Ones to assist humanity in awakening their heart centers.
You can receive the love of the Great Ones into your heart
centers to further awaken them. You can radiate the love of
the Great Ones to humanity, assisting in bringing about a
consciousness of love and oneness that will lead to finding
solutions for world problems.

The celebration of love takes place in the soul plane.
Because there is no time here, you can come to this celebration
at any time, and you will be entering just as it is occurring.
The power of a group to assist the Great Ones in awakening
the heart centers of humanity increases with each person who
joins in. All of you who come will act as receivers and
transmitters of the love that the Great Ones send to humanity.

To become a part of the celebration of love and to call
upon the Great Ones, travel to the Temple on the soul plane.
Go to the middle of the courtyard and call your soul to you.
Feel its loving presence. Move into a state of soul love as you
circulate energy among your heart centers. Feel the serenity

of love. Breathe in and lift energy from your heart to your head center, feeling your harmony with all souls. Breathe out and join with your soul to stimulate the hidden point, increasing your will to love humanity and all life. Breathe in again, lifting solar plexus energy into your heart center and then into your head center, surrendering those desires that stop you from loving. Watch as light moves among your heart centers faster and faster, until you can no longer follow the movement. The light circulating among your heart centers becomes an electric, glowing, radiant light. Your primary heart center becomes an enormous orb of light extending well beyond your body. You are filled with soul love. You feel your connection to the Universal Presence of Love.

Meet the souls of all who are here. Start by greeting the souls of all who are reading this book and participating in this celebration of love. All of you are creating a beautiful, shimmering, radiant heart light. Imagine linking your primary heart center with the heart center of everyone here. Everyone here offers you love and makes a heart connection with you. Observe how the size of this group grows every time you come here, for every day more and more people are awakening their heart centers and joining you.

There are millions of people who are working to bring about an awakened humanity. I will call these people *lightworkers*. Look out over the sea of light in the soul plane and sense the souls of other lightworkers. They may appear as points of light that shine out as you think of them. Invite the souls of all lightworkers on the planet to join with you to call upon the Great Ones to awaken the heart centers of humanity. Feel thousands, then tens of thousands of lightworkers responding by joining you. You are forming an enormous group. You are not alone in thinking that there is a better, more compassionate, more cooperative way to live, a way that is in harmony with the earth and all life. Changes come about when those of you who feel this way join together. Feel the strength, power, and light in the group that is now forming on the soul plane to call upon the Great Ones. Invite anyone else you can think of to join with you, including the souls of your friends, family, and loved ones. Make a heart connection to link them with the larger group that is forming.

> *Call upon the Great Ones*
> *to awaken the heart centers*
> *of humanity.*

The celebration of love is beginning. All of you here join to send out a call to the Great Ones to assist humanity. Do so by feeling your love for humanity. From the depth of your being, desire a better life for everyone on the planet. Discover your enormous capacity for love as you join with others to work for the good of humanity. It is your love for humanity and the strength of your desire for humanity to evolve that calls the Great Ones. Everyone present now concentrates on asking the Great Ones to assist humanity. Everyone sets aside individual desires and concerns and focuses on loving and caring for humanity.

The Great Ones begin to gather, starting with the Beings of Light, Masters, and Enlightened Ones. Watch as Beings of Light gather here from many higher dimensions, including the Being of Love who supported you as you blended with your soul and awakened your heart centers. All the Beings of Love that each of you has worked with join the celebration now. The Being of Love you have been connecting with asks you, "Are you ready for this step? Are you ready to express more love than you have ever known? Are you ready to be a source of love to others through your thoughts, actions, and words? Are you ready to awaken your heart centers through loving humanity and all life?" To use the energy that the Great Ones send, you will need to be willing to do your best to express love, wisdom, and compassion; to practice the qualities of soul love; and to become an example of love for others. When you are ready, say, "I accept this opportunity to make a contribution to humanity."

Everyone joins together now to send a call to those Great Ones who are even more evolved than the ones already present. The Beings of Love sound a note of love. It is a note that carries many overtones and harmonies. This note is so rich that it spans many dimensions, touching the souls and hearts of all. The higher communities join in, followed by the souls of all who are here. This call gains in strength and power. Join with everyone present to call upon the Great Ones who can transmit powerful energy to assist humanity in awakening its heart centers. You may want to sound an "om" to contribute your note to the call to the Great Ones.

This group call is so powerful in its intent to call the Great Ones that it draws their attention. Observe as they hear the call that everyone is making to them. They focus their attention on all of you.

### *Receive love from the Great Ones into your heart center.*

There is a long, profound silence. It is almost as if the universe has paused in its breath. Time stands still. The Great Ones gather to themselves the love that will be transmitted to all of you who are participating in this celebration of love. Through you this love will reach humanity.

The Great Ones start their transmission of love. They are joined by all the Masters, Beings of Love, and Enlightened Ones, who add their love to the transmission. A surge of magnetic, radiant love is sent to you who have accepted this opportunity. Receive this transmission into your primary heart center. Distribute this powerful energy of love through your heart centers, moving even more deeply into a state of soul love. Your ability to become one with the Universal Presence of Love and to know yourself as a loving being increases.

The Great Ones next send an amplifying love to increase all the love that is within you, waiting to emerge. Their broadcast amplifies the special frequencies of love that are yours to bring to humanity, so that you may better know the unique gifts of love that are yours to offer. Say to yourself, "I recognize and honor the love that is within me. I know it is one of my most important gifts to humanity."

The Great Ones send you another transmission of love to assist you in recognizing the love that is all around you from moment to moment, strengthening your connection to the Universal Presence of Love and all the love within you. Receive this emanation of love into your heart center. Say to yourself, "I find love in every moment. I walk the path of love." As you grow more skilled in finding the love in every situation and in every moment, you assist others in awakening their heart centers.

The Great Ones send you another transmission of love to aid you in increasing your potential for love in this lifetime. Receive this love and say to yourself, "I open to my potential for love. At every moment my potential to receive and radiate love increases." Desire your potential for love to grow so that you can become an even more powerful force of good and a source of love for humanity and all life. Recognize how your doing this is part of your higher purpose of receiving light and radiating light to others.

The Great Ones send one final transmission of love to assist all of you in releasing the past. If you are carrying any shame or guilt, if you feel bad about things you have done that were not as high and loving as you would have liked, or if you have any painful or unpleasant memories, self-judgments, or regrets, you can give these to the Great Ones to transform. If there are any situations you have been replaying in your mind, wishing you had done something better or said something differently, let go of them now. When you release pain, you add to the positive energy available to everyone.

*S*ay to yourself,
*"Today is the first day*
*of a new life of love."*

Put your hand over your heart, and receive a transmission from the Great Ones to release your past and any pain that you feel because of it. As you receive their love, say to yourself, "I now release the past with love." The Great Ones have enormous compassion. They take your pain into themselves and transform it into love. Receive love back and use it to fill up the places that contained your pain. As you turn your past over to the Great Ones and receive their broadcast of love, places in your heart that have been closed can open. You have even more love to offer humanity.

As your heart centers awaken, imagine that you are lifting the veils and letting your heart light be visible to your family, friends, and acquaintances. Many of you hid the light and love within you when you discovered that the people around you did not know how to respond to it. It is time to lift the veils and to be seen for the wise, loving, and compassionate person you are. Picture how you might be able to make an even greater contribution to humanity if you were willing to be seen more fully for who you are. Let your heart light be visible to everyone you know. You might picture yourself taking off layers of coats, sweaters, and clothes, symbolically unveiling the love and light within you. As you receive transmissions of love from the Great Ones, your heart center becomes the most radiant it has ever been. It is a beautiful orb of light, a small star or sun, whose rays of light go far beyond your body, touching every living thing around you with the radiance of love.

*Feel the power and light available*
*as you join with other lightworkers.*

Now that you are filled with the love of the Great Ones, radiate love to, and receive love back from, all the lightworkers who are here with you. Imagine yourself in perfect harmony with other lightworkers. Your work enhances their work and their work enhances yours. Each of you is playing your part in the grand plan. As you link with other lightworkers, you can tap into the love and support that is available through this connection. You are making important connections on the soul plane that can bring many new and wonderful people into your life. There are enough of you to make a difference, and the world is already beginning to change for the better because of you.

You are ready to radiate the love of the Great Ones to humanity. Imagine love spiraling out through all your heart centers to those who are most receptive to it. The light of love is being turned on all over the world. First a few hearts awaken, then more and more, until there is a shimmer of heart light all around the world. Love spreads throughout the world, wrapping the globe in the iridescent light of love.

Most of the problems facing humanity, such as war, poverty, and hunger, could be solved with enough love. As more people awaken their heart centers, greed will turn into sharing, competition will turn into cooperation, and people will begin taking responsibility for solving the problems facing humanity. Changes in humanity will come first as inner changes—through soul contact and awakened heart centers.

The crises facing humanity are teaching people to work together and offering people chances to awaken their heart centers as they do. Humanity is developing group consciousness as the presence of love grows stronger. Many people are becoming aware that they are part of a greater whole. As humanity reaches for solutions to their challenges, people will create shared visions, cooperate to bring them about, and take actions that put the good of the whole above the needs of any one individual or nation.

Appreciate the importance of what you are doing. All of you present are accepting a greater role in humanity's evolution as you receive love from the Great Ones and radiate it to humanity. There will be a time when this process reaches critical mass and millions of people's heart centers will awaken. Positive changes will come about more quickly than you might think possible. Thank the Great Ones for their response and support. Sound a final "om" as you imagine people's heart centers awakening and love spreading throughout the world.

# A Celebration of Love

# Soul Play

Rejoin the celebration of love often to call on the Great Ones and receive their transmissions of love. Each time, blend with your soul, circulate energy among your heart centers, and experience all or some of the steps that follow.

1. Journey to the soul plane and go to the Temple. Make a heart connection to all the groups of people here, including those who are reading this book, all lightworkers, and everyone else.

2. Join with everyone at the Temple to call the Great Ones by sounding an "om." As the Great Ones respond, receive their magnetic, radiant love into your heart center. Next receive their transmission that amplifies the special frequencies of love that are yours to bring to humanity. Say, "I recognize and honor the love within me."

3. Accept the transmission that allows you to find love in the moment and that strengthens your connection to the Universal Presence of Love. Say to yourself, "I find love in every moment. I walk the path of love."

4. Absorb the transmission that increases your potential for love. Say, "At every moment my potential to receive and radiate love increases."

5. Receive the transmission that assists you in releasing the past. Feel your heart opening in places that have been closed. Say, "I now release the past. Today is the beginning of my new life of love."

6. Radiate love to humanity. Let love spiral out through your heart center to those who are most receptive. Watch as more hearts awaken, wrapping the globe in the iridescent light of love.

# CHAPTER 21

# Making Wheels of Love

*You build wheels of love to bring soul love,*
*harmony, and higher purpose to all those with whom you connect.*
*You create right relationship with everyone.*

You have learned how to soul link, circulate light and energy among your heart centers, and move into a state of soul love. You have called upon the Great Ones and received their transmissions of love into your heart center. You are now ready to learn how to make heart connections with many people at once through making wheels of love. Creating a wheel of love is a way to radiate soul love to groups of people with whom you are connected. You can make a wheel of love when you are physically present with groups of people, or at any time simply by thinking of them. You can create wheels of love with your family, friends, neighbors, and an office, social, or sports group. You can make wheels of love everywhere you go to bring love to and to be in harmony with everyone you are around. You can create a wheel of love to bring higher purpose into a group situation. By making a wheel of love you can lift and expand all the patterns of light between you and others, making them more beautiful. You can expand into the oneness of love and become one with the Universal Presence of Love, offering this love to others. You can assist everyone in the group who can resonate with your broadcast in having a higher, more flowing, and more harmonized connection to one another.

*Receive the gifts of love
your family has to offer you.*

You can make a wheel of love with everyone in your family, bringing higher purpose, harmony, peace, and love into all your family connections. You can offer those who are ready an opportunity to go to their next stage of heart awakening. You can gather in the essence of love from past generations, and send this essence to future generations.

Travel to the soul plane and blend with your soul. Look out over the sea of light, and call to you the souls of family members: children, parents, brothers and sisters, spouse or partner, grandparents, aunts, uncles, cousins, nieces, nephews, and so on. Do not try to identify which soul belongs to which person. Picture all of their souls coming as you call, forming a circle around you. Sense the souls of all these people; then pay attention to their heart centers.

Circulate energy among your heart centers. Feel the serenity of love as you lift energy from your heart center into your head center, expanding your love. Watch as your soul stimulates the hidden point, strengthening your will to love everyone in your family. Lift solar plexus energy up to your heart center, releasing any power struggles. As your heart light grows more beautiful, imagine you are merging with the Universal Presence of Love that brings love to all. Picture rays of light coming out from the golden orb of your heart center, touching the heart center of everyone who has formed a circle around you. It is as if you are in the center of a wheel. Rays of light coming from your primary heart center to other people's heart centers form the spokes of this wheel. Feel the

Solar Light above you. Call its light to you, observing as it sends a ray of light down through your head center to your heart center. Solar Light moves out from your primary heart center to everyone in the circle around you, adding its light of higher purpose to all your connections. It assists your soul in making the patterns of energy between you and your family members more beautiful, harmonious, and loving.

Radiate a soul-love quality, such as an accepting, amplifying, or transparent love, through this wheel of love. Think of the special frequencies of love that are yours to bring to humanity, and radiate your love to all your family members. Radiate the love that you received from the Great Ones to your family. Picture everyone giving you permission to be fulfilled and happy, sending you their support and blessings. Send them your support and hold a vision of everyone in your family becoming successful, fulfilled, and enlightened.

In the soul plane you can broadcast love to and receive love from the souls of your ancestors. Call the souls of your ancestors to you and imagine them joining in your wheel of love. They send you all the best of everything they have learned as souls. Receive their love for you. You are part of the future generation they had a role in creating. Open to all their gifts of love.

Sense the essence of love that is special to your family line; it is one of the reasons you chose to be born in your family. Call to you the souls of future generations. Create a wheel of love with them. Radiate to future generations the essence of love that is part of your family lineage. Broadcast to them all the gifts of love your ancestors have just given you. Imagine that your family—past, present, and future—is creating a beautiful pattern of light made out of the combined light of each of your souls. Ask your soul and the Solar Light to dissolve anything that hides this light, so that the essence of love becomes clearer and more beautiful with each generation.

## *Create wonderful relationships with all your friends.*

You can make a wheel of love to have more harmonious, nurturing, and loving connections with all of your friends. On the soul plane, call the souls of all of your current friends. The Solar Light is above you, sending a ray of light down through your head center to your heart center. Love and light move out from your primary heart center to all of your friends, creating a wheel of love. If you are experiencing conflicts with friends, send your soul's will to love to stimulate the hidden point in your solar plexus center, and lift energy from your solar plexus center into your heart center.

Resolve that you will experience your soul's serenity with all of your friends, and that you will stay in your center of love no matter what is going on in their lives or yours. Pick several qualities of soul love to radiate that you would like to experience more of when you are with your friends, such as serenity, expansion, love, or compassion. Radiate forgiveness to everyone, feeling the serenity that comes from acceptance and unconditional love. Radiate the love of the Great Ones to all your friends to assist them in awakening their heart centers. Expand into the oneness and feel the Universal Presence of Love all around you. As you do, you are offering this connection to everyone with whom you are making a wheel of love.

As you make a wheel of love, those who can respond to your love will come closer, until you are surrounded by those who can receive your love, resonate with it, and match it. You can have wonderful relationships with all of your friends. Call to you the souls of future friends. Watch as they join in your wheel of love. Radiate love to everyone and receive love as it comes back to you. The love you receive back increases the love you have to give. As you make this wheel of love you are attracting new friends into your life who can receive and respond to the love that you have to offer.

## *L*ift group energy with a
## wheel of love.

You can create a wheel of love and radiate soul love to any group you are a part of, such as a social, community, sports, office, or church group. The people involved might be your associates, neighbors, employers, employees, or colleagues. You can make the wheel of love when you are by yourself, meditating, or at a conference, party, or a gathering of any kind.

Work with the Solar Light and create a wheel of love whenever you want to link a group of people in higher purpose and to make the patterns of light between you and the group more beautiful. Create a wheel of love to lift and evolve group energy. You can broadcast the love you received from the Great Ones if it feels appropriate. You can make the wheel of love to help fulfill the soul reasons and the practical reasons you came together as a group.

Think of a group of people with whom you would like to create a wheel of love. Connect with your soul. Distribute energy among your heart centers and move into a state of soul love. Feel your soul's serene, unconditional, accepting, and transparent love. Sense how your soul lifts, expands, unites, and connects all energies. Let your will to love grow stronger, and lift the energy from your solar plexus center into your heart center to transform any power struggles into love. Receive rays of light from the Solar Light into your heart center, and radiate love to others through your wheel of love. Make a picture that all your connections with this group will reflect the love you are now capable of receiving and radiating.

Do not expect any immediate or measurable results. However, pay attention and note any changes in yourself or in the relationships you have with group members during the next few days and weeks. You may discover wonderful changes in your group connections. Note any shift in the effectiveness of the group, in people's ability to work together, to have more clarity about group goals, and so on.

If you are working with the wheel of love to bring harmony to a difficult environment or situation and nothing improves or changes, you can know that you have added all the love this group can hold. You will need to decide if you want to continue to connect with this group, finding peace with things as they are. Or, you may want to find another group to work with which can respond to soul love, or whose purpose is more in alignment with yours.

## *Be in harmony with everyone in your neighborhood and city.*

Make a wheel of love with all your neighbors and everyone in your city to be in harmony with them. Link your heart center with the heart centers of the people on your street, in a small area around you, or in your apartment building. Broadcast love to all your neighbors through your wheel of love. Mentally send your blessings to your neighbors, no matter how you feel about them. Desire the best for everyone. At various times, such as when you are walking down a street or entering your home, take a moment to make the wheel of love and to radiate soul love to all your neighbors.

Make the wheel of love with everyone in your city or area. By broadcasting soul love and Solar Light through your wheel of love, you can assist in making the patterns of light more beautiful between you and the souls of everyone in your city.

The souls of those people who are receptive to the love you are radiating will send love back to you. Your love is transparent; it passes right through those who are not receptive without adding any of its own characteristics or any of your individual energy. As you make the wheel of love and radiate love to everyone in your city, you are drawing to yourself opportunities to meet new friends, to have better interactions with people, and to fulfill part of your soul's purpose of offering love to others.

*Be in harmony with all life.*
*Make wheels of love*
*everywhere you go.*

Make wheels of love everywhere you go to add light and love, and to be in harmony with everyone around you. Make a wheel of love with people when you are in a store, restaurant, theater, airport, hospital, or any other public place. Create wheels of love at a seminar, meeting, or any other kind of gathering. Always remember to put the Solar Light above you, so that you are distributing energy from a higher source than yourself and your soul. You can invite the Being of Love into your heart center to radiate this high, refined love to others, especially when you are around people or situations that need more harmony, love, healing, or peace. Broadcast your special frequency of love to humanity. Feel the Universal Presence of Love all around you, offering this energy to others so that they may be more aware of their connection to this presence of perfect love.

You may or may not notice results from making wheels of love with people. Sometimes you will find people responding in wonderful ways, and other times you will only have an inner sense of increasing love, serenity, and expansion that tells you your love is being received. Creating wheels of love is a wonderful way to be in harmony with the universe and to add light to any group of which you are a part.

Remember as you soul link and create wheels of love that you are planting seeds of love that will emerge and blossom in their own timing. It may take days, weeks, or months for the changes you are creating as you work in this way to become your reality. Your relationships *will* change for the better. Do not worry if your relationships do not change over-night. Day by day and moment by moment you are making new choices that will eventually show up as visible, noticeable, and positive changes in your connections with others. Major changes are usually the culmination of many thousands of smaller actions and decisions. Be patient and know that all the soul love you are radiating will eventually bring about important and positive changes in your relationships with others.

# Soul Play

Pick a group of people from the list below with whom to make a wheel of love.

- Your current family, ancestors, and future generations.
- Your past, present, and future friends.
- A group you are a part of, such as your office, sports, or church group, and so on.
- Your customers, clients, or students.
- Your neighbors and people in your area or city.

Make a wheel of love by blending with your soul, merging your heart center's jewel with your soul's jewel. Circulate energy and light among your heart centers until your primary heart center is radiant with love. Observe as rays of light move out from your heart center and touch the heart centers of everyone in the group.

1. Focus on the Solar Light as it comes down through your head center and goes out to everyone in the group, making the patterns of light between you and others more beautiful.
2. Radiate various qualities of soul love, such as an amplifying, transparent, soft, enduring, accepting, and harmonizing love.
3. Radiate the love of the Great Ones to the group.
4. Connect with the Universal Presence of Love and offer this connection through your wheel of love.
5. Bring the Being of Love into your heart center and radiate this refined, evolved love to others.
6. Radiate the special love that is uniquely yours to bring to humanity.

# Chapter 22

# Radiating Love

*You join with the Beings of Light and other lightworkers
to radiate love. You become a more beautiful and perfect light
as you radiate love to others.*

You have received the transmissions of the Great Ones and made wheels of love to radiate love to others. You are ready to work with the Masters, Enlightened Ones, and Beings of Light to radiate love to humanity, to groups of people in need, to children, and to other kingdoms. Working with the Beings of Light to radiate love to those who are evolving or who are in need is one of the most powerful and rapid ways you can choose to awaken your heart centers.

To join with the Beings of Light to radiate love, you do not need to make wheels of love. You are no longer in the center of the wheel, receiving and distributing love to others. Instead you are joining other lightworkers to assist the Beings of Light through radiating love to various groups, humanity, and other kingdoms. As you join with the Beings of Light who are helping a certain group, you can radiate soul love, letting the Beings of Light direct your love to wherever it will do the most good.

You can work with the Beings of Light to radiate love whenever you choose. You can radiate love as a part of your daily meditation or during special times when assistance is needed, such as during a local or world crisis. Once you have radiated love, ask what outer work is appropriate, if any, in order for you to give form to the inner work you have done. Inner work does not take the place of outer action if action is indicated. It is important to do the soul work of radiating love first, for as you do you can more easily discover the appropriate outer forms and actions. Sometimes after you have worked soul-to-soul, no action or outer work will be called for. At other times there may be many actions which appear valid for you to take.

## *Join with the Beings of Light to radiate love during a world crisis.*

You can radiate love to aid those involved in a local or international emergency, such as a war, earthquake, volcano, fire, flood, or hurricane. If you feel drawn to assist at such a time, take a moment to sit quietly and send soul love to those who are involved. Connect with your soul and circulate energy among your heart centers. Move into a state of soul love and feel your connection to the Universal Presence of Love. Unite with all the Beings of Light and lightworkers who are assisting with this particular crisis. Imagine that soul love is pouring through your heart center to all those affected by this crisis. Your love is added to the reservoir of spiritual energy being generated. The Masters and Beings of Light who are working with this group will direct your love to exactly where it is needed.

If you are the one in a disaster area or experiencing an emergency, repeat the same process. Blend with your soul. Lift any fear, anxiety, or other unwanted energies you might be absorbing from your environment into your heart center. Circulate energy among your heart centers, moving into a state of soul love. Receive the transmissions of calm, reassuring love being sent to you from the Beings of Light and lightworkers who are broadcasting love to everyone affected by this situation. Feel the Universal Presence of Love that is always present. Tell yourself, "I am safe and protected wherever I am." Invite the Being of Love into your heart center. After you receive love, radiate love to everyone in your area who needs support and comfort. Connecting with all the love that is being broadcast is a wonderful way to stay calm, and to know that you are safe and protected no matter what is happening around you.

Reach out to your community and help on the physical plane in whatever way calls to you. Group events such as floods, fires, earthquakes, or wars provide many opportunities to practice love. People are often more open to receiving love and are better able to express the love within them during such times.

If you are in need of help, or have lost your possessions or a home, practice receiving love and letting others give to you. Know that for everything that leaves your life, something better is coming. Affirm that there is a higher purpose for what is happening, even if you do not understand it yet. Hold the thought that good will come out of this event and look for all the good within it.

> *Radiate love to lift the conditions*
> *of those in need.*

You can work with the Beings of Light to radiate love to groups of people who are in need of assistance, support, or encouragement. Or, you can ask for guidance about where your broadcast of soul love will do the most good. Some Beings of Light are working with people to support them in blending with their souls. Others are radiating love to the hearts of all who are open to receive it. Still other Beings of Light are dispelling the fear and negative thoughts that encircle the planet, while others are birthing new thoughts of love and cooperation. Some Beings of Light are working from the soul plane to promote global peace or to alleviate hunger.

There are many groups you can send love to. You can radiate soul love to people in hospitals, or to those who are ill, dying, or suffering. You can radiate soul love to the homeless, drug addicted, or abused. If you have received solicitations from a charitable organization and would like to assist in an important way, radiate love to that organization. Imagine your magnetic heart light assisting such organizations in attracting all the love, assistance, and resources they need to fulfill their higher purpose. You can join with the Beings of Light to radiate love to any group of people as a part of your path to enlightenment and as a powerful way to awaken your heart centers. You might want to think of a group to radiate soul love to, then join with the Beings of Light and radiate soul love to that group.

## Surround children with soul love.

There are many children on the planet at this time, and many more are being born at every moment. Your love can make a difference in their lives. You can surround all children with soul love to assist them in finding and fulfilling the higher purpose of their lives. Take a moment to close your eyes and think of children. Join with your soul, circulate light and energy through your heart centers, and broadcast love to children simply by thinking of them. Picture joining with other lightworkers to mentally send children and newborns a message: "We welcome you and thank you for all the light you are bringing to this world. We recognize who you are and support you in creating your higher purpose. You are not alone. You are part of a wonderful group of lightworkers, and we are here, surrounding you with love." Send whatever other messages you feel are appropriate as you surround their souls with your love, support, encouragement, and protection.

When you are with children, soul link and take a moment to sense their souls. Mentally tell them that you recognize who they are, and radiate soul love to them. Notice what responses children make to your inner messages. Perhaps they will take a deep breath, look you in the eye, or open up in some way as they receive the love you are sending. Even if there is no noticeable change, your transmission of love and your recognition of who they are is a great gift to all children.

## *Realize your potential for love by loving humanity*

To become a point of light through which the Great Ones can work, your love needs to be inclusive and tolerant. As you expand your love to all of humanity, you increase your ability to make a contribution to a larger and larger group of people. Practice expressing tolerance and inclusiveness toward all those you meet or think of. Erase the concepts of "us" and "them" from your thoughts. Catch yourself whenever you think of people in ways that label them as different from you. Imagine that anyone you have labeled as an "outsider" is your friend, including people of a different culture, religion, race, or country; people who hold opposing beliefs and opinions; and people who act in ways you do not approve of. What would the world feel like to you if all these people were no longer outsiders but friends? They would all be people to love. You have an enormous capacity to love. You may find it easier than you have imagined to include all of humanity in your loving thoughts.

Take a moment to think of a group you feel opposes the things you believe in. Can you radiate your love to the members of this group, even though you may not agree with their views? Can you open your heart and sense your shared humanity, the similarity of your daily worries and concerns? If you have trouble radiating love to these people, imagine connecting with their souls on the soul plane. Explore how easily you can harmonize, connect, expand, and add light to your relationship with them at this level.

Reflect on your life and your activities. Are there places where you have created an "us/them" in your life, such as at your workplace, in a social group, or within your circle of family and friends? Look at how you might let go of any barriers that separate you from others. Do not force yourself to feel loving and inclusive. Love any feelings you have that separate you from others, and keep lifting them into your heart center.

Join with the Beings of Light to radiate love to humanity and to feel your oneness with all people. Picture everyone growing wiser, more loving, and more connected to their souls, for this is what is happening. Rather than despair at the way people act, see that all people are doing the best they know how. They have not yet fully awakened their heart centers and are not aware of the Universal Presence of Love. Practice loving humanity, including people's faults and weaknesses, as well as their strengths and beauty. As you learn to love humanity, you will be able to more easily love yourself.

## Assist the animal kingdom in evolving.

Part of humanity's higher purpose is to aid other kingdoms, such as the animal kingdom, in their evolution. You can use the same techniques to connect with and send soul love to animals that you used to radiate love to people. Animals have souls and heart centers. You can soul link with them, connect with their souls, and broadcast all the soul-love qualities you have learned.

In addition to radiating love to individual animals, you can work with the entire animal kingdom. Or, you can work with specific groups, such as bears, cats, dogs, birds, dolphins, whales, farm or laboratory animals, butterflies, reptiles, or insects. You may want to ask your soul to show you what group can most benefit from your love, or is part of your path to work with.

Start by thinking about what type of animal you want to work with. Radiate soul love as you have learned, joining with the Beings of Light and lightworkers who are assisting the animal kingdom in its evolution. If you have selected a certain type of animal to work with, ask to join with the Beings of Light who are in close communication with and working for the evolution of this group of animals. Imagine love spiraling out from your heart center. You are sending soul love to these animals to assist them in taking their next evolutionary steps, in lifting their pain and suffering, and in transforming their fears. As you do, the Beings of Light who are working with this group will distribute your love and light wherever it can do the most good. Envision a world that supports these animals in having a wonderful life, full of joy, growth, and love.

## Support plants in their evolution.

Part of the higher purpose of humanity is to assist the plant kingdom in its evolution. Plants evolve by creating new species and by achieving greater beauty. Blend with your soul, move into a state of soul love, and join with the Beings of Light who work closely with the plant kingdom to assist them in their evolution. Take a moment to radiate love to all the trees, grasses, flowers, and plants in your area. Pay attention to the plants around you, and note all the beauty they add to your life and to the world. Extend your awareness farther and farther out, sensing plants all around the world. Expand even more, until you are in touch with the soul of the plant kingdom. Join your love with that of the Beings of Light to send love to the soul of the plant kingdom. As you broadcast soul love to the plant kingdom, surround it with love and vitality. Picture it as strong and healthy.

## *E*mbrace the soul of the earth with your love.

Take a moment to feel your love for and connection to the earth. Think of the mountains and deserts, the beaches and grassy plains. Picture the earth's rocks and minerals, its oceans, lakes, and rivers, and its layers of air. What a wonderful living being the planet Earth is! Sense the soul of the earth. It is an enormous, radiant light, much larger than the souls of individual people. Greet the soul of the earth and radiate love to it. Feel its love coming back to you. Ask if there is anything you could do right now at the soul level to assist the earth. After you radiate love to the soul of the earth, let ideas come into your mind about changes you could make to live a life that is in greater harmony with the earth.

## *R*adiate love to the Great Ones.

Take time to thank the Beings of Light, Masters, Enlightened Ones, and Great Ones for their constant, committed, and steady love for you and for all of humanity. Every time you think of it, send a thought of gratitude to them and appreciate them for all they are doing. Take a moment to do this right now. Close your eyes, connect with your soul, and circulate energy among your heart centers. Feel the love that is all around you as you join with the Universal Presence of Love. Let your love radiate outward on this field of love to all those Beings who are steadily radiating love to humanity. Feel their caring, compassion, and dedication. Thank them every day, or as often as you remember. Observe what happens to your heart centers, your experience of your soul, and your ability to radiate love as you do this.

## *Receive all the gifts that come back to you as you radiate love.*

You now have all the tools you need to be in right relationship with everyone in your life. You know how to get into a state of soul love and connect with the Universal Presence of Love. From this state you can experience harmony with others through your actions and words. You can serve and empower others to grow stronger, wiser, and more whole. You are becoming a force of good and a source of light. When you express soul love consistently and reliably, all the other gifts of your soul can come to you. Expressing soul love opens the door for your soul to give you its gifts of vision, insight, revelations, and knowledge. You can tap into the higher powers of your soul, for you can now be trusted to use them for the good of the whole, without harm to yourself or to others.

Being in right relationship with people and embracing love does not mean that everything around you will be perfect and that everyone will love you all the time. What it means is that *you* will love all the time. You will be unaffected by the turmoil of others. You will be untouched by the places where other people's hearts are not yet open, for you will be at peace in your own heart. You will be able to experience love no matter what is happening around you.

Soul love is more than how you act. You become the sun that warms and nurtures. You become the light that lights the way. You become the stillness that opens doors. You become the love that heals. You become the softness that soothes. You know you are part of the Universal Presence of Love. Your love releases any chains of fear, limitation, and the past. Your love opens gateways to the future; releases the hidden potential; and adds the light that allows all that is good to emerge, blossom, and come into being. Resolve to be at peace with the world and everyone in it. Feel your oneness with all life. Say to the universe, "I love you, I am one with you, I am in harmony with all life." Know yourself as a being of love, as a soul, and as a Spirit, for that is who you are.

# Soul Play

Pick one of the following groups to radiate love to, or any others that come to mind. To radiate love, blend with your soul and circulate light among your heart centers. Connect with the Universal Presence of Love. Join with the Beings of Light and all lightworkers who are working with this group. Imagine love spiraling out from your primary heart center, adding to the love that is being transmitted to those in need. As you unite with others to radiate love, you are making one of the most important contributions you can make to bring about an awakened humanity. Choose one group to radiate love to right now:

- People involved in a local or world crisis.
- Those in need, such as people in hospitals; those who are dying, suffering, or homeless; or any other group that comes to mind.
- Ask the Beings of Light what group they would like assistance with instead of picking your own. Radiate love to whatever group comes to mind after you ask.
- People in a position of influencing others, such as world leaders, spiritual teachers, and so on.
- Humanity, including all children.
- The animal kingdom.
- The plant kingdom.
- The planet Earth.
- The Masters, Enlightened Ones, and Great Ones.
- Acknowledge yourself for the love you radiate, your willingness to grow, and for your contribution to humanity as you awaken your heart centers.

# *Teaching the* Soul Love *Book*

You are welcome to hold classes, form study groups, and share the processes used in this book with others. As you have been reading this book, you have been meeting with others on the soul plane who are making soul contact and awakening their heart centers as you are. Because you have made these inner linkages, you may now be feeling the urge to bring these inner connections into outer form. Meeting together with others to meditate, to share, and to call upon the Enlightened Ones can be an important part of your awakening and a wonderful way to make a valuable contribution to humanity. (Any meeting of three or more people is considered a group.)

You are living in a time of enormous change and transformation. Humanity is awakening rapidly. Group work will be the keynote of the coming millennium. Groups provide the Enlightened Ones with the greatest opportunity to assist each individual as well as humanity. No one individual can fully receive their enormous energy. It is only when you join with others and call upon them together that they can send you a more complete broadcast of love, light, and energy. Many of the Enlightened Ones can only be reached with a group call. That is why you have been joining with others on the soul plane, in the celebration of love, and at other times.

You do not need to be a master of the principles contained in the *Soul Love* book to teach or facilitate group meetings. You do need to be committed to exploring and implementing these tools of love in your daily life. Take a moment to get quiet, and let your soul speak to you about the appropriateness of gathering people together to discover more about soul love. Let insights come to you in the next days and weeks. Explore the role you want within a group. Do you want to lead, be a facilitator, or join an existing group?

When you sense it is time to gather or find a group, journey to the soul plane and meet the souls of your potential group members. Distribute light among your heart centers and become the magnetic quality of soul love. Make a wheel of love with these souls, radiating the qualities of love that are yours to bring to humanity. Invite people who are responsive to your light and who want to be a part of the group you are forming to come into your life. Work with the Solar Light to bring its light of higher purpose into your connection with everyone who will be joining you. If you want to join an existing group, ask to be guided to these people at the soul level and make a wheel of love with them.

After you have made these inner connections, create a vision of the higher purpose of your group gathering. In addition to studying the *Soul Love* book, you might want to be more specific about your higher purposes for gathering together. Your higher purposes might be to make soul contact, to awaken your heart centers, to create soul relationships, to attract soul mates, and to receive and radiate love to humanity and various groups. Write out your vision. Look at this vision and energize it as you create a wheel of love with the souls of those people you are magnetizing to come to your group meetings.

Work with your soul to decide on a class or study group format. Determine the number of weeks you will meet, how long each meeting will be, and when you will meet. You may want to go through the chapters of this book and determine the key points you want to study, such as soul contact, soul linking, awakening each heart center, distributing energy among all three heart centers, creating soul relationships, attracting a soul mate, and working with the Great Ones. Be patient and let the form of your class evolve as you create wheels of love with the souls of those who will be coming.

Once you have decided on the higher purpose of your classes and know the format and what you will be studying, follow your inner guidance about what outer action to take to attract this group. You may be drawn to posting notices at a local bookstore, or inviting friends to meet and study this book. Continue to blend with your soul, make wheels of love, magnetize students, and trust that when the timing is right a class will come together.

I would like you to have the freedom to develop your own class format, so I am not setting any guidelines for a class structure. However, I do have some suggestions that can greatly enhance your group connections. You may follow these suggestions based on your wisdom about the appropriateness of these steps for the group you have attracted.

I suggest that you start your classes by asking group members to make an inner connection with me, asking for a transmission of my energy. Make blending with your soul and connecting with the Beings of Light and the Solar Light an important part of each class. It is usually best to start with a meditation, either led by you or someone else in the group, or by playing one of my guided meditation tapes. My tape albums, *Soul Love: Awakening Your Heart Centers* and *Creating a Soul Relationship* contain guided meditations made to go with this book that can be played during group meetings. Some people design one class around each tape, play the tape, and discuss their experiences afterward. It is often best to save talking and sharing for after a meditation, for then your personality interactions will reflect more of the soul connection you have just made.

To further develop your capacity to feel and express soul love, you can work together on the Soul Play processes. You may want to ask people to read certain portions of the book before coming to class, or read the book out loud during group meetings. Include time at the end of each class to radiate love to humanity and to various groups you choose; this is an important way to distribute all the energy you have gathered. When you send love to others you will be able to receive even more energy and love from the Enlightened Ones.

As a group leader or facilitator, use and practice the soul-love qualities in this book with your class. Be as inclusive, tolerant, noncritical, and loving as you can be. Soul link with everyone in the group, and let your personality connection evolve from this inner linkage. If there are personality challenges with group members, use these as opportunities to experience the power of the new tools of love you have learned. Soul link and lift solar plexus energy into your heart center to transform any conflicts or challenges.

Be the best leader you can imagine. Honor your commitments to those who come to your class, such as preparing, starting and ending on time, and holding classes when you say you will. Ask those who come to commit to doing the same. If you are attending a class, follow these suggestions as well. Give your love and support to your group leader.

As a group leader, you may find people asking you questions and expecting you to have answers. Instead of providing answers and solutions, encourage group members to receive answers for themselves by blending with their soul and asking for its guidance. Support each other as a group in finding your answers through soul contact. Rather than giving advice, you can empower others by asking them, "What do you think your soul would do in the situation you find yourself in?"

I do have a few requests I would like you to honor when you are holding classes or forming study groups based on this book. Please teach the material by following what is presented here as closely as possible; do not change the images or the qualities of the heart centers. I ask that you not make audio-cassette tapes of any of the processes in this book to distribute to others or make publicly available. (It is fine to record audio-cassette tapes of the Soul Play or other book processes solely for your personal use.)

I and the Beings of Light send you our love. We will join you as you link with others to become points of light and love through which we can pour our love. At the moment you decide to gather a group, energy will be sent to you to assist you. All you need do is ask, and open to receive. We will be with you through every step of your journey of being a teacher, facilitator, or group member. Remember that your students are also your teachers. We welcome you as a fellow traveler on the path of love and look forward to our continued soul connection with you.

—Orin

Note: If you would like to buy multiple copies of this book or the audio-cassette tapes that go with this book for your classes, contact *LuminEssence* for more information. Orin has made various guided meditation tapes that can be used with each section of this book. For instance, the tape album *Soul Love: Awakening Your Heart Centers* can be used with Sections I and II. The album *Creating a Soul Relationship* can be used with Section III, and the tape *Celebration of Love* can be used with Section IV. (See the back of the book.)

—Sanaya

# What's Next?

You have finished reading this book and taken a major step on your spiritual journey. If you are wondering what to do next, take a moment to get quiet and ask your soul for guidance about your next steps of spiritual growth. Ask what areas you could grow in that would assist you in expressing more of your soul's light, love, and presence in your daily life.

If you would like to deepen your experience of your soul and further awaken your heart centers, review the chapters of this book that call to you. Practice the Soul Play exercises that draw you. In addition, Orin has made audiocassette guided meditations to assist you in more directly experiencing your soul and the love and light that is possible as you awaken your heart centers.

Orin's higher purpose in being present at this time is to serve through offering people a path of spiritual growth in various areas of their lives. The books and tapes by Orin listed in the following pages were created to assist you in growing spiritually through awakening your heart centers, through creating a soul relationship and attracting a soul mate, and through working with the Solar Light. Orin also offers tapes and books to assist you in learning how to channel, to create prosperity and abundance, to know your soul's joy, to develop your personal power, to grow spiritually, to be your higher self, and more.

As you look through the following pages, notice if any area appeals to your heart and your sense of play and adventure. If so, let this be a message from your soul about the next area to put energy into that will allow your soul to express more of its love and light through you. Whatever area you choose to grow in, and whatever forms you choose to assist you in your growth, commit to your spiritual growth. Make fulfilling your potential and expanding your consciousness a priority in your life, for it is your greatest gift to yourself and the most important contribution you can make to the oneness of which you are a part.

# ORIN BOOKS AND TAPES

In addition to making information available through books, Orin has also created many audiocassette guided meditation tape courses. Orin feels that listening to guided meditations, when your mind is in a relaxed, open state, is one of the most powerful and effective ways known to create lasting changes in your life. As you listen you will work with your soul, higher self, conscious mind, and subconscious mind to create positive results in any area you focus on.

Orin has carefully selected the words, images, and processes on the tapes to assist you in reaching expanded states of consciousness where you can more easily access all the wisdom, love, and light within you. In these heightened states you can view your life from a larger perspective, receiving many insights and revelations. As you listen you can take wonderful journeys of light, discovering the richness of your mind and the incredible inner experiences you are capable of having. Orin hopes each guided meditation will provide you with a delightful, enjoyable, and relaxing way to transform your consciousness, as well as to increase your ability to sense the subtle energy of your guide, to receive energy from the Beings of Light, and to know and experience your soul.

To assist you in experiencing the higher dimensions of light as you listen to Orin's journeys, Sanaya has produced music with an angelic guide called Thaddeus to bring you the melodies, harmonies, and music of the soul plane. The purpose of this music is to assist you in liberating yourself from the bonds of matter, in healing your emotional body, in awakening your higher mind, and in moving into the higher vibration of your soul. The music is paced to relax your body and slow your breathing, opening doorways into higher states of awareness. Thaddeus' music, combined with Orin's voice and energy, leads you to wonderful experiences of light, joy, bliss, peace, and love as you listen and expand into all that you are capable of being.

# Soul Love
## Awakening Your Heart Centers

As you listen, you will receive energy from Orin, the Beings of Light, and the Being of Love. All these Beings will join you to assist you in awakening your heart centers. Experience more deeply the love, joy, and peace of your soul.

*Side 1: **Making Soul Contact** –* Meet your soul, receive its love, and travel into your soul's jewel, the essence of your being.

*Side 2: **Blending With Your Soul** –* Blend your heart center's jewel with your soul's jewel. Dissolve, transform, and evolve those energies within you that do not reflect your true being.

*Side 3: **Soul Linking** –* Soul link to radiate love and transform your relationships. Recognize when your love is being received, intensify your broadcast of love, and know when to stop radiating love.

*Side 4: **The Serenity of Love** –* Radiate the magnetic, amplifying, transparent, accepting, and unconditional qualities of soul love.

*Side 5: **The Oneness of Love** –* Awaken your head center and connect with the oneness of which you are a part. Make the energies between you and others more beautiful.

*Side 6: **The Will to Love** –* Activate the hidden point and feel your soul's consistent, steady, soft, patient, and forgiving love.

*Side 7: **Surrendering to Love** –* Lift Solar plexus energy into your heart center. Free yourself from responding to negative energy, let go of power struggles, and stay in your center.

*Side 8: **Soul Love** –* Circulate light between your heart centers to awaken them and to move into a state of soul love.

Set of 4 tapes, 8 meditations by Orin with beautiful music by Thaddeus. *Specify **SL105** **$59.95***

*Note: Purchase the *Creating a Soul Relationship* tape album (*see next page*) at the same time and save $19.95. *To order both, specify **SL107** **$99.95***

## Improve Your Relationships

Single tapes below by Orin contain music by Thaddeus, and the same journey on both sides so you can replay without rewinding.
Subpersonality Journeys: **I Am Loved, I Am Lovable** *SI105 $9.98*
or **Overcoming the Self-Destruct** *SI060 $9.98*
**Achieving Intimacy – Opening Your Heart** *RE005 $9.98*
**Compassion and Forgiveness** *SI104 $9.98*
**Having What You Want in a Relationship** *RE003 $9.98*
**Letting Go of a Relationship** *RE004 $9.98*

# Creating a Soul Relationship

Use the guided meditations on this audiocassette tape course to go beyond the skills you learned in this book. Play together as souls and create a soul relationship with someone you love as you listen. Increase the light and love between you at the soul level that can then manifest as wonderful changes in your daily life together.

*Side 1: **Meeting Soul to Soul*** – Journey to the soul plane, blend with your soul, and meet and play with the soul of the person with whom you are creating a soul relationship.

*Side 2: **Light Play*** – Radiate light to another person's soul, balance and harmonize the way your souls' lights work together, and bring the clear light of your soul connection into your daily life.

*Side 3: **Love Play*** – Join with your soul to awaken your heart center, soul link with a loved one, and play together as souls to transform your relationship with love.

*Side 4: **Discovering the Higher Purpose of a Relationship*** – Explore the reasons you are in a relationship with someone and create a vision of your higher purposes in being together.

*Side 5: **Creating the Relationship You Want*** – Work with the universal laws of relationship and create the relationship you want.

*Side 6: **Dissolving Obstacles to Love*** – Love and appreciate yourself, keep your heart open, be vulnerable, and release conflict.

*Side 7: **Discovering New Ways to Love*** – Release relationship patterns you have learned from your parents, update the images others hold of you, and recognize the greatness in yourself and others.

*Side 8: **Soul Blending*** – Blend souls with a loved one to increase the light in both of your souls. Create light where there was none before as you become like two suns or stars together.

Set of 4 tapes, 8 meditations by Orin with beautiful music by Thaddeus. *Specify **SL106** $59.95\**

*\*Note: Purchase the* Soul Love: Awakening Your Heart Centers *tape album at the same time and save $19.95. To order both, specify **SL107** $99.95*

## Celebration of Love

**Celebration of Love:** Side 1 of this tape will guide you to call upon the Great Ones, receive their powerful transmission of love into your heart center, and radiate love to assist the Great Ones in awakening the heart centers of humanity. **Making Wheels of Love:** Side 2 will guide you to make wheels of love to transform your relationships with family, friends, and groups. *SL001 $12.50*

# Solar Radiance *Tape Course*
## Becoming a More Perfect Light

This is one of Orin's most advanced tape albums. You will be guided to experience expanded states of consciousness, learn how to birth a consciousness of light, and work with Solar Light to manifest with light. This course is for you who are ready to create profound changes in your consciousness, in your spiritual path, and in your daily life. You will bring Solar Light into your circumstances, projects, relationships, and activities to enhance all the light that is there, and to release anything that is not light. Orin transmits some of the light body energies in these journeys.

*Side 1: Increasing Your Radiance* – Expand your consciousness and align with the Solar Light to become a more perfect light.

*Side 2: Transforming Your Life With Light* – Work with the qualities of Solar Light to transform any circumstance, situation, or blockage.

*Side 3: Creating More Light About You* – View the people and situations in your life from a higher level and add light to them.

*Side 4: Birthing Light and Awareness* – Find your next steps and discover new ideas, directions, and answers.

*Side 5: Becoming a More Perfect Light* – Work with three Masters to expand your ability to align with the Higher Will and to express the creative intelligence within you.

*Side 6: Liberating the Light Within* – Release old thoughts, beliefs, and dense emotions. Become more aware of your inner guidance.

*Side 7: Condensing Light Into Matter: Manifesting With Light* – Find those things you want to manifest as they exist as light. Learn how to condense light into matter to bring them into your daily life.

*Side 8: Building a Solar Consciousness* – With a Solar consciousness you can learn to find and use the light in every moment.

Set of 4 tapes, 8 meditations by Orin in attractive album. Tapes contain beautiful music by Thaddeus. *SL104 $49.95*

## Angelic Music to Receive Solar Light
### Solar Light Transmissions

This music by Thaddeus, an angelic being channeled by Sanaya, can assist you in experiencing and receiving Solar Light. This music calls to you a Master of Light who will transmit Solar Light to you as you listen. With his music, Thaddeus summons the violet angels to you for cellular transformation, the yellow angels to build a finer nervous system that can handle more light, the rose angels to add Solar Light to your heart and circulatory system, and the deep blue angels to heal whatever needs healing. 2 audiocassette tapes, 4 musical journeys in album. (Tapes contain music only.) *MS205 $29.95*

# *Attracting Your Soul Mate* *Tape Course*

These guided journeys by Orin will assist you in attracting a soul mate. You can use the meditations in this album to connect with your soul mate at the soul level, prepare yourself to meet your soul mate, release any negative beliefs that have kept you from having a soul mate, and invite your soul mate to come into your life.

*Side 1: Making Soul Contact* – Make a stronger connection to your soul, then find and connect with the souls of potential soul mates.

*Side 2: Meeting Soul-to-Soul* – Decide what you want in a soul mate, then find the soul of the person you are asking for.

*Side 3: Learning About Your Soul Mate* – Learn more about the person you have met at a soul level. What is this person looking for in a relationship?

*Side 4: Exploring the Possible Relationship* – Go into the future and explore what a relationship might be like with this person.

*Side 5: Preparing for Your Soul Mate* – Let go of beliefs that may be blocking you from having this soul-mate relationship.

*Side 6: Talking to Your Inner Advisor* – Look deep within to discover if you really want a soul mate. Let your inner advisor talk to you.

*Side 7: Subpersonality Journey* – Work with and transform that part of you that may be resisting a soul-mate relationship.

*Side 8: Calling in Your Soul Mate* – Call your soul mate to you. Celebrate your union; have your relationship energized by the Masters.

Set of 4 tapes, 8 meditations by Orin in attractive album. All tapes contain meditative music by Thaddeus. *SL102 $49.95*

*Attracting Your Soul Mate* – Guided meditation by Orin to meet and play with your soul mate on the soul plane, then magnetize your soul mate to come into your life. Music by Thaddeus. Same journey is on both sides. *RE002 $9.98*

## *Transformation: Evolving Your Personality*

As you awaken your heart centers, you may find you need to work with your personality to handle the challenges that come from being on an accelerated path of spiritual growth, such as blockages, doubts, mood swings, old issues coming up, overstimulation, and so on. Meditations include: **Self-Appreciation, Honoring Your Path of Awakening; Focusing Inward – Hearing Your Soul's Voice; Focusing Upward – Hearing the Voice of the Masters and Guides; Reparenting Yourself – Changing the Past; Creating the Future With Light; Beyond Intellect – Opening Your Higher Mind; and Journey to the Temple of the Masters to Reprogram at a Cellular Level.** Set of 4 tapes, 8 meditations in attractive album. Music by Thaddeus. *SG200 $49.95*

# Living With Joy *Book*

*Living With Joy*, the first book of Orin's Earth Life Series, teaches you how to know and express the joy of your soul. You will learn how to sound your soul's note of joy, so you can grow with joy and release pain and struggle. You will explore ways to feel inner peace no matter what is happening around you, experience the unlimited freedom of your soul, change negatives into positives, trust your inner guidance, take a quantum leap, gain clarity, open to the new, and increase your capacity to receive. You will explore how to live in higher purpose and find your life purpose. You will discover more ways to feel secure and balanced, to improve your self-esteem, to know your value and worth, and to feel the joy of your soul in your everyday life. (H J Kramer, 216 pages) *LWJ* $12.95

## *Experience Your Soul's Joy* *Meditation Tapes*

*Living With Joy–The Path of Joy,* Volume I: Audiocassette course by Orin to sound your soul's note of joy and bring more joy into your life. Meditations include: **Finding Your Path of Joy; Changing Negatives Into Positives; The Art of Self-Love; Self-Worth and Self-Esteem; Power – Refining Your Ego; Knowing Your Heart's Wisdom; Opening to Receive;** and **Appreciation and Gratitude.** Set of 4 tapes, 8 meditations in attractive album. Meditation music by Thaddeus. *L201* $59.95*

*Living With Joy–Taking a Quantum Leap,* Volume II: Audiocassette course by Orin. Meditations include: **Finding Inner Peace; Balance and Stability; Clarity – Living in the Light; Freedom; Embracing the New; Taking a Quantum Leap; Living in Higher Purpose;** and **Recognizing Life Purpose.** Set of 4 tapes, 8 meditations in attractive album. Meditation music by Thaddeus. *L202* $59.95*

*Purchase both Volumes I and II (L201 and L202) at the same time and save $19.95. *To order both, specify L203* $99.95

**Other guided meditations tapes by Orin to assist you in growing with joy:** (Single tapes below contain music by Thaddeus and same journey on both sides, except where indicated.)
*Living With Joy:* Audiocassette tape to go with the book:
Side 1 – Affirmations; Side 2 – Guided Journey. *L100* $9.95
*Opening to Receive:* Allow things to come easily to you. *L106* $9.98
*Taking a Quantum Leap:* Speed up time, keep your balance while you take a major leap forward in any area of your life. *L103* $9.98
*Feeling Inner Peace:* Feel peaceful no matter what is happening in your or others' lives. *L101* $9.98
*Self-Love:* Learn to love and appreciate yourself. *L102* $9.98

# Personal Power Through Awareness Book

*Personal Power Through Awareness,* the second book of Orin's Earth Life Series, teaches you how to experience true personal power, the power that comes from being in touch with your soul, with the souls of others, and with the guidance that is available from the higher dimensions. You can leave the denser energies, where things are often painful, and live in the higher energies where you can feel more loving, calm, focused, and positive. Using these processes, you can increase your awareness of the energy around you. With this enhanced awareness you can choose how you want to act and feel, develop your intuition, become aware of your inner guidance, and send and receive telepathically. (H J Kramer, 216 pages) *PPTA $12.95*

## Know Your Soul's Power Meditation Tapes

*Personal Power Through Awareness – Sensing Energy, Volume I:* Audiocassette tape course by Orin. Learn how to create the reality you want using energy, thought, and tools of light. Develop your skills of visualizing. Sense and affect the energy around you, increase your intuitive abilities, and receive higher guidance. Meditations include: **Sensing Energy; Sensing Unseen Energy; Sensing Energy in Others; Who Am I? – Sensing Your Own Energy; Developing Intuition; Evolving Emotional Telepathy; Sending and Receiving Telepathic Images; and Receiving Higher Guidance.** Set of 4 tapes, 8 meditations in attractive album with music by Thaddeus. **P201 $59.95***

*Personal Power Through Awareness – Journey Into Light, Volume II:* Audiocassette tape course by Orin. Create the future you want in various areas of your life. Experience yourself in new, higher ways, learn how to love yourself more, come from your power, stay in your center around others, and more. Meditations include: **Learning Unconditional Love; Handling Pain – Transforming Negative Energy; Bringing Your Unconscious Into Consciousness; Journey Into Light – Going Higher; Self-Love – Evolving Your Inner Dialogue; Transforming Your Inner Images; Finding Your Deepest Truth; and Wisdom – Being Your Higher Self.** Set of 4 tapes, 8 meditations in album, music by Thaddeus. **P202 $59.95***

*Purchase both Volumes I and II (P201 and P202) at the same time and save $19.95. To order both, specify P203 $99.95

*Personal Power Through Awareness,* audiocassette tape to go with the book: Side 1 – Affirmations; Side 2 – Guided Journey. Contains beautiful music by Thaddeus. *P100 $9.95*

# Spiritual Growth _Book_

## Being Your Higher Self

**Spiritual Growth,** the third book of Orin's Earth Life Series, teaches you how to develop an integrated, balanced personality called your higher self, one who knows and can follow the goals and purposes of your soul. You will learn how to link with the Higher Will to flow with the universe; connect with the Universal Mind for insights, enhanced creativity, and breakthroughs; receive revelations; and see the bigger picture of the universe. You will learn non-attachment, right use of will, and how to lift the veils of illusion. You will discover how to expand and contract time, to choose your reality by working with probable futures, to become transparent to energy you do not want to resonate with, and to be your higher self. This book will help you align with the higher energies that are coming, using them to live the best life you can imagine for yourself. (H J Kramer, 252 pages) _SG_ _$12.95_

## Be Your Higher Self _Meditation Tapes_

**Spiritual Growth** – _Raising Your Vibration, Volume I:_ Guided meditations for: **Raising Your Vibration, Calming Your Emotions, Accelerating Your Spiritual Growth, Choosing Your Reality, Expanding and Contracting Time, Lifting the Veils of Illusion, Right Use of Will,** and **Becoming Transparent.** Set of 4 tapes, 8 meditations in album; music by Thaddeus. **_SG101_ _$59.95*_**

**Spiritual Growth** – _Being Your Higher Self, Volume II:_ Guided meditations for: **Being Your Higher Self, Creating With Light, Connecting With the Universal Mind, Linking With the Higher Will, Seeing the Bigger Picture, Opening Awareness of the Inner Planes, Allowing Your Higher Good,** and **Non-Attachment.** 4 tapes, 8 meditations in album, music by Thaddeus. **_SG102_ _$59.95*_**

*Purchase both Volumes I and II (SG101 and SG102) at the same time and save $19.95. _To order both, specify_ **_SG103_ _$99.95_**

Single tapes below contain beautiful music by Thaddeus and the same journey on both sides (except where noted).

**Spiritual Growth,** audiocassette tape to go with the book:
Side 1 – Affirmations; Side 2 – Guided Journey. _SG100_ _$9.98_
**Being Your Higher Self** _SI040_ _$9.98_
**Age Regression** _SI041_ _$9.98_
**Past-Life Regression** _SI043_ _$9.98_
**Creating Your Perfect Day** – _Wake Up Meditation_ _SI101_ _$9.98_
**Learning to Relax** _SI026_ _$9.98_

# Opening to Channel *Book*

## How to Connect With Your Guide

This book will assist you in making a connection with and learning how to channel a guide or your higher self. Channeling is a skill that can be learned. Sanaya and Duane, with the assistance of their guides, Orin and DaBen, have successfully trained thousands to channel using these safe, simple, and effective processes. You will learn how to tell if you are ready to channel, how to attract a high-level guide, and how to go into trance. You will explore how guides transmit messages and communicate with you, and will develop your skill as a receiver and translator. You will learn how to give readings and how to look into probable futures for yourself and others. You can channel knowledge, personal and spiritual guidance, healing techniques, and more. (H J Kramer, 264 pages) *OTC $12.95*

### Opening to Channel *Audiocassette Tape Course*

These tapes are a wonderful companion to the *Opening to Channel* book. They contain the processes taught by Sanaya and Duane at their opening to channel seminars. As you listen, Orin and DaBen will join their energy with yours and lead you through each step of channeling, including relaxation, concentration, sensing life-force energy; mentally meeting your guide; a guided journey to verbally channel your guide (including questions to ask your guide); trance inductions; and guided meditations to learn how to give yourself and others a reading. Four tapes with over 16 processes in cassette album. *C100 $49.95*

### Advanced Channeling Skills *Seminar on Tape – Recorded Live*

This audiocassette channeling course will teach you how to use your connection to your guide to channel on your and others' past-lives; emotional, mental, and physical energy bodies; and chakras. You will explore mind linking and future traveling through the centuries to increase your visionary abilities. Sanaya and Duane talk about channeling. 4 tapes in album. *W007 $49.95*

### Improve Your Channeling *Seminar on Tape – Recorded Live*

You will learn to channel information on your and others' life purposes, parental programming, relationship patterns, higher purposes of a relationship, and the higher purpose of your job or daily activities. This course also contains talks by Sanaya and Duane about commonly asked questions such as how you can gain more confidence in your channeling, let go of doubts, and more. 4 tapes in album. *W006 $49.95*

**Meeting Your Spirit Guide:** A beginning journey to meet your guide and receive advice. (Same journey on both sides.) *O14 $9.98*

*If you need to increase your manifesting skills, change your beliefs about abundance, or discover more about what you want and how to draw it to you, the following will assist you.*

# *Creating Money* Book
## *Keys to Abundance*

*Creating Money* is a book to guide you step-by-step to creating money and abundance. It was given to Sanaya Roman and Duane Packer by their guides, Orin and DaBen. Learn the spiritual laws of abundance, advanced manifesting techniques, and how to draw to you your life's work. Use your magnetic will to draw to you what you want. Come out of survival, value yourself and your work, and join with your soul to create abundance. Expand your thinking, change your beliefs, open to receive, and follow your heart and inner guidance to experience greater abundance in your life. Create money as a source of light for yourself and others. You can work with energy to create what you want and tap into the unlimited abundance of your soul and the universe. (H J Kramer, 288 pages)  *CM $12.95*

### *Creating Money* Audiocassette Tapes
Orin has made these meditations to assist you in increasing your prosperity consciousness by reprogramming your subconscious mind. Journeys include: **1–Magnetizing Yourself; 2–Clearing Beliefs and Old Programs; 3–Releasing Doubts and Fears; 4–Linking With Your Soul and the Guides; 5–Aura Clearing, Energy, and Lightwork; 6–Awakening Your Prosperity Self; 7–Success: Releasing Fear of Success, Failure, Going for It!; and 8–Abundance: Creating Plenty in Your Life.** Four tapes, eight meditations by Orin in attractive album with music by Thaddeus. *M100 $49.95* These tapes are available as single tapes for $9.98 each title. (Single tapes contain same journey on both sides.)

### *Abundance Affirmation Cards:* 112 Creating Money affirmations
on blue-linen cards. Pull one everyday for your daily prosperity affirmation. *CMA $12.95*

### *Abundance Affirmations* Audiocassette Tape by Orin: Side 1 contains
the affirmations from the book *Creating Money.* Side 2 contains a powerful magnetizing technique. *M001 $9.98*

### *Becoming a Writer* Tape Course
These powerful meditations contain the processes given to Sanaya by Orin to help get their books out to the world. Meditations include: **I Am a Writer, Manifesting Your Writing, Loving to Write, Connecting With Your Audience,** and processes to get your writing published. Set of 2 tapes, 4 meditations in album. Music by Thaddeus. *SI016 $29.95*

# Advanced Manifesting and Magnetizing
### Seminar on Tape by Orin and DaBen – Recorded Live

Orin and DaBen, a guide channeled by Duane Packer, present a twelve-step manifesting process that has created powerful results for people who have used these processes. In this live seminar on tape, you will pick one thing you want to manifest, and then turn what you want into energy, bring it into your DNA, utilize the power of your emotions to draw it to you, open to receive, work with your higher self and the Beings of Light to discover more about your life purpose, magnetize what you want, and expand and contract time.

Learn how to open to the unlimited abundance of your soul and higher self, expand your consciousness, and draw to you what you want. Set of 4 tapes in attractive album with many guided meditations by Orin and DaBen. *W005 $49.95*

# Becoming a World Server *Tape Course*

This audiocassette tape course can assist you in discovering and creating your life purpose, changing or launching your career, and opening to a greater level of success in your work.

*Side 1:* **The Awakening: What Am I Here to Do?**
*Side 2:* **Sounding Your Note** – Tune into the plan of humanity and join your note with it. Awaken the qualities you will need to succeed.
*Side 3:* **Expanding Your Vision** – Clear blockages, see the bigger picture of your work, believe in yourself, and develop right timing.
*Side 4:* **Meeting Your Spiritual Community** – Learn how to call upon all the assistance that is available from the higher realms.
*Side 5:* **Calling to You Those You Can Serve** – Call to you your students, clients, or customers.
*Side 6:* **Navigating the Flow** – Learn how to draw to yourself opportunities, to make right choices, and to develop clear vision.
*Side 7:* **Being a Source of Light** – See yourself as a leader. Draw to you those whose higher purpose is to help you carry out your work.
*Side 8:* **Becoming a World Server** – Dedicate your work to the light.
Set of 4 tapes, 8 meditations by Orin in attractive album. Tapes contain beautiful music by Thaddeus. *M200 $49.95*

# Get Your Work Out to the World *Tapes*

These single-tape meditations by Orin contain music by Thaddeus and the same journey on both sides.

**For Self-Employed People:** Attract business, clients, sales, and money. *SI037 $9.98*
**Public Recognition:** Magnetize people to your work. *SI015 $9.98*
**My Perfect Career:** Find your perfect career. *SI058 $9.98*
**Opening Creativity – Attracting Ideas** *SI046 $9.98*

# Awakening Your Light Body: Keys to Enlightenment
## *A Six-Volume Audiocassette Tape Course*
### *by DaBen and Orin*

Orin joins with DaBen to present *Awakening Your Light Body*, a tape course with extensive written material and six audiocassette tape albums to take you on a step-by-step spiritual growth program. This course is recommended for those of you who have been on a growth path for a while, and who want to experience many heightened, expanded states of consciousness, take a quantum leap, and increase your ability to sense the subtle energies of your soul and the soul plane. This course has created positive life changes and results beyond anything we imagined for ourselves and others.

## What Is Your Light Body?

Many of you are in the process of making the evolutionary leap of awakening your light bodies. Your light body is an energy body that exists at a higher level, closer to your soul, than your chakras.

As you awaken your lower energy body centers, you can regulate the amount of energy you take in from your environment, change less harmonious energies into higher ones, and use the energy around you to go higher. As you awaken these centers, you may experience a stronger sense of personal power and a greater ability to control your emotions, stay centered, release old blocks and stuck emotional energy, and respond with love and compassion.

Your upper centers open doorways to the higher realms of light, such as the soul plane. Awakening them assists you in adding light to your thoughts, opening your channel upward, and connecting with the Universal Mind. There are three light body centers besides the lower and upper energy body centers. As you awaken these centers, you become a radiating source of light. You can more easily choose those actions that reflect the light of your soul and higher self. You can experience many illumined states of awareness. These states of consciousness can feel deeply insightful, blissful, and take you beyond thought into direct experiences of beingness. You will be able to see, sense, or feel the expanded, more beautiful energies of the higher dimensions and make them a part of your daily life.

## *Call or Write for a Free Subscription to Our Newsletter*

To receive a FREE subscription to Orin's newsletter/catalog with further information about the *Awakening Your Light Body* course as well as about other Orin tapes and seminars, write to *LuminEssence Productions*, P.O. Box 19117, Oakland, CA 94619.

*LuminEssence Productions • P.O. Box 19117 • Oakland, CA 94619*
*To order by phone with Visa/Mastercard call (510) 482-4560*

# Order Form

BUY THREE $9.98 TAPES AND GET A FOURTH $9.98 TAPE FREE!!
*(Free tape offer does not apply to tape albums.)*

Your Name _____
*(Please print)*

Address _____

City _____ State _____ Zip _____

Country _____

Telephone: Home (_____) _____ Work (_____) _____
*(In case we have any questions about your order.)*

| QTY | ITEM | DESCRIPTION | PRICE |
|-----|------|-------------|-------|
|  |  |  |  |
|  |  |  |  |
|  |  |  |  |
|  |  |  |  |
|  |  |  |  |
|  |  |  |  |
|  |  |  |  |

| **Shipping and Handling** | **U.S.A.** | | **International Air Mail** | | | | |
|---|---|---|---|---|---|---|---|
| Subtotal: | First Class Mail | U.P.S. | Canada | Europe | Other International | Subtotal | |
| Up to $10 ... | $2.75 | $4.60 | $3.75 | $5.70 | $6.90 | Shipping | |
| $11 to $50 ... | $4.15 | $5.10 | $7.30 | $11.00 | $14.50 | TOTAL | |
| $51 to $89 ... | $5.50 | $5.50 | $8.30 | $13.65 | $18.85 | | |
| $90 to $100 ... | $7.05 | $6.95 | $9.55 | $19.80 | $24.35 | | |
| $101 to $200 ... | $8.30 | $8.10 | $14.60 | $28.90 | $39.90 | | |
| Over $200 ... | $9.85 | $9.25 | $18.45 | $40.70 | $52.75 | | |

☐ Check here if you prefer your order shipped UPS.
*(UPS cannot deliver to P.O. Box addresses.)*

*Thank You for Your Order!*

Payment enclosed: ☐ Check ☐ Money Order
Please charge my: ☐ Visa ☐ MasterCard

Credit Card No. _____ Exp. Date _____

Signature as on card _____

Please make check payable to **LuminEssence Productions**. Remember to allow time for U.S. Mail or UPS delivery after order is shipped. All orders shipped within two business days of receipt. Incomplete orders will be returned. **International orders** payable in U.S. Funds drawn ON a U.S. bank. All international orders will be shipped by air mail.     H1

# About the Author

Sanaya Roman has been channeling Orin, a timeless being of light, for over fifteen years. A Phi Beta Kappa graduate of the University of California at Berkeley, she has studied the metaphysical sciences for years. Orin has offered thousands of people a path of spiritual growth, soul contact, and expanding consciousness through books, tapes, and seminars.

Sanaya has worked with Orin to write *Living With Joy, Personal Power Through Awareness,* and *Spiritual Growth.* She and Orin have coauthored the books *Creating Money* and *Opening to Channel* with Duane Packer, who channels a guide named DaBen.

Sanaya currently conducts seminars with Duane Packer in awakening the light body and in spiritual growth. She is writing the *Awakening Your Light Body* book with Duane Packer, and working with Orin on his next book in the Soul Life Series to be called *Soul Vision.* She produces the *Birth Into Light* newsletter/catalog, with articles on spiritual growth, light play processes, and information on Orin tapes and books. Sanaya resides in the Pacific Northwest.

## *Please Note!*

Sanaya and Orin are putting their time and energy into group work, feeling this is the most powerful way to create a shift for people. To provide this opportunity for group work, Sanaya leads seminars with Duane Packer and his guide DaBen to assist people in awakening their light bodies and in growing spiritually. Sanaya does not offer individual sessions. If you would like to receive energy from Orin and Sanaya, join them during the Sunday morning meditations. (See next page.)

# Join Orin for Sunday Morning Meditations

Sanaya: Many of you throughout the world are studying Orin's work. I want to thank all of you for your support of Orin, and offer you an opportunity to continue our soul connection, by inviting you to join Orin and me on the inner planes on Sunday mornings. Orin and I meditate and focus light upon you if you ask for it and are open to receive it. Experience the light and transformation that is possible as thousands meditate together on the inner planes. Bring your soul's light to any area of your life that you focus on. Deepen your connection to the Beings of Light and other lightworkers. Orin and I will transmit to all of you who join us on Sunday mornings from 9:15 to 9:30 AM, California time. (Or, join us at 9:15 to 9:30 AM your time and we will create light together that will move around the world.) For more information about how to participate, send for our newsletter.

## Join Us for Our Worldwide Meditations

Join with Orin and DaBen, a guide channeled by Duane Packer, to participate in our global linkups. At least once a year we ask everyone to join us who wants to call upon the Great Ones and request their assistance for humanity. During this time, thousands join together on the inner planes to call upon and receive energy from the Great Ones. These are enlightened Beings of Light who are in touch with the highest forces of light. They work from the higher dimensions of light, transmitting powerful energy that can assist humanity in bringing about positive changes. We have called upon the Great Ones to assist us in awakening our heart centers, changing thoughts of scarcity into thoughts of abundance, and in growing through joy rather than through pain and struggle.

---

### For a Free Subscription to Orin's Newsletter

If you would like more information about the Sunday morning meditations or the upcoming worldwide meditations, call or write for a free subscription to Orin's newsletter/catalog. This contains messages from Orin as well as information about other books, tapes, and seminars. Write to *LuminEssence Productions*, P.O. Box 19117, Oakland, CA 94619; or call (510) 482-4560. Be sure to include your name, address, and phone number.

# The Journey Continues

As you have read this book, made soul contact, and awakened your heart centers, you have taken a wonderful journey of growth, discovery, and transformation. As with any journey, when you return you may find that your view of your life is expanded, enriched, and fuller. You have a greater appreciation of what you already have in your life and of who you are.

You have returned from your journey with many gifts. Some are gifts of love you received from the Beings you met that you now carry in your heart. Some are inner images that have added to the richness of your mind. Some gifts are healing tools and skills that you can add to those you already know and practice. Some are gifts of song that you can listen to, hearing new melodies of joy and peace within your heart.

You are different now from when you started your journey. Your world has grown larger. You have a new vision of who you are and more love and compassion for yourself and others. You have brought back many gifts of love that you can share with others. You can relive your journey, reviewing and remembering all the wonderful times you had and the unique places you visited. You can discover and integrate all the love and riches you have returned with. Every day you gain some new insight about what you have learned, realizing that your journey will continue to enrich and expand your life forever.